Theodore Roosevelt

Also by Louis Auchincloss
in Large Print:

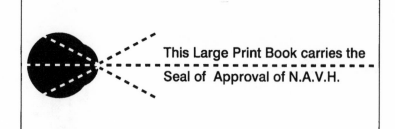

This Large Print Book carries the
Seal of Approval of N.A.V.H.

Theodore
Roosevelt

Louis Auchincloss

Thorndike Press • Waterville, Maine

Published in 2002 by arrangement with
Henry Holt and Company, LLC.

Thorndike Press Large Print Biography Series.

The tree indicium is a trademark of Thorndike Press.

The text of this Large Print edition is unabridged.
Other aspects of the book may vary from the original edition.

Set in 16 pt. Plantin by Myrna S. Raven.

Printed in the United States on permanent paper.

Library of Congress Cataloging-in-Publication Data

Auchincloss, Louis.
    Theodore Roosevelt / Louis Auchincloss.
      p. cm.
    Originally published: New York : Times Books, 2002,
in series: The American presidents series
    ISBN 0-7862-4135-7 (lg. print : hc : alk. paper)
    1. Roosevelt, Theodore, 1858–1919. 2. Presidents —
United States — Biography. 3. United States — Politics
and government — 1901–1909. 4. Large type books.
I. Title.
E757 .A88 2002b
973.91′1′092—dc21
   [B]   2001059671

FOR JOHN AND TRACY

Editor's Note

The American Presidency

The president is the central player in the American political order. That would seem to contradict the intentions of the Founding Fathers. Remembering the horrid example of the British monarchy, they invented a separation of powers in order, as Justice Brandeis later put it, "to preclude the exercise of arbitrary power." Accordingly, they divided the government into three allegedly equal and coordinate branches — the executive, the legislative, and the judiciary.

But a system based on the tripartite separation of powers has an inherent tendency toward inertia and stalemate. One of the three branches must take the initiative if the system is to move. The executive branch alone is structurally capable of taking that initiative. The Founders must have sensed this when they accepted Alexander Hamilton's proposition in the Seventieth Federalist that "energy in the executive is a leading character in the definition of good government." They thus envisaged a strong president — but within an equally strong system of constitutional accountability. (The term *imperial presidency* arose in the 1970s to describe the situation when the balance between power and accountability is upset in favor of the executive.)

The American system of self-government thus comes to focus in the presidency — "the vital place of action in the system," as Woodrow Wilson put it. Henry Adams, himself the great-grandson and grandson of presidents as well as the most brilliant of American historians, said that the American president "resembles the commander of a ship at sea. He must have a helm to grasp, a course to steer, a port to seek." The men in the White House (thus far only men, alas) in steering their chosen courses have shaped our destiny as a nation.

Biography offers an easy education in American history, rendering the past more human, more vivid, more intimate, more accessible, more connected to ourselves. Biography reminds us that presidents are not supermen. They are human beings too, worrying about decisions, attending to wives and children, juggling balls in the air, and putting on their pants one leg at a time. Indeed, as Emerson contended, "There is properly no history; only biography."

Presidents serve us as inspirations, and they also serve us as warnings. They provide bad examples as well as good. The nation, the Supreme Court has said, has "no right to expect that it will always have wise and humane rulers, sincerely attached to the principles of the Constitution. Wicked men, ambitious of power, with hatred of liberty and contempt of law, may fill the place once occupied by Washington and Lincoln."

The men in the White House express the ideal and the values, the frailties and the flaws, of the voters who send them there. It is altogether natural that we should want to know more about the virtues and the vices of the fellows we have elected to govern us. As we know more about them, we will know more about ourselves. The French political philosopher Joseph de Maistre said, "Every nation has the government it deserves."

At the start of the twenty-first century, forty-two men have made it to the Oval Office. (George W. Bush is counted our forty-third president, because Grover Cleveland, who served nonconsecutive terms, is counted twice.) Of the parade of presidents, a dozen or so lead the polls periodically conducted by historians and political scientists. What makes a great president?

Great presidents possess, or are possessed

by, a vision of an ideal America. Their passion, as they grasp the helm, is to set the ship of state on the right course toward the port they seek. Great presidents also have a deep psychic connection with the needs, anxieties, dreams of people. "I do not believe," said Wilson, "that any man can lead who does not act . . . under the impulse of a profound sympathy with those whom he leads — a sympathy which is insight — an insight which is of the heart rather than of the intellect."

"All of our great presidents," said Franklin D. Roosevelt, "were leaders of thought at a time when certain ideas in the life of the nation had to be clarified." So Washington incarnated the idea of federal union, Jefferson and Jackson the idea of democracy, Lincoln union and freedom, Cleveland rugged honesty. Theodore Roosevelt and Wilson, said FDR, were both "moral leaders, each in his own way and his own time, who used the presidency as a pulpit."

To succeed, presidents must not only have a port to seek but they must convince Congress and the electorate that it is a port worth seeking. Politics in a democracy is ultimately an educational process, an adventure in persuasion and consent. Every

10

president stands in Theodore Roosevelt's bully pulpit.

The greatest presidents in the scholars' rankings, Washington, Lincoln, and Franklin Roosevelt, were leaders who confronted and overcame the republic's greatest crises. Crisis widens presidential opportunities for bold and imaginative action. But it does not guarantee presidential greatness. The crisis of secession did not spur Buchanan or the crisis of depression spur Hoover to creative leadership. Their inadequacies in the face of crisis allowed Lincoln and the second Roosevelt to show the difference individuals make to history. Still, even in the absence of first-order crisis, forceful and persuasive presidents — Jackson, Theodore Roosevelt, Ronald Reagan — are able to impose their own priorities on the country.

The diverse drama of the presidency offers a fascinating set of tales. Biographies of American presidents constitute a chronicle of wisdom and folly, nobility and pettiness, courage and cunning, forthrightness and deceit, quarrel and consensus. The turmoil perennially swirling around the White House illuminates the heart of the American democracy.

It is the aim of the American Presidents

11

series to present the grand panorama of our chief executives in volumes compact enough for the busy reader, lucid enough for the student, authoritative enough for the scholar. Each volume offers a distillation of character and career. I hope that these lives will give readers some understanding of the pitfalls and potentialities of the presidency and also of the responsibilities of citizenship. Truman's famous sign — "The buck stops here" — tells only half the story. Citizens cannot escape the ultimate responsibility. It is in the voting booth, not on the presidential desk, that the buck finally stops.

— Arthur M. Schlesinger, Jr.

Introduction

Theodore Roosevelt is one of the few presidents whose life, or at least the public image of his life, is even more important historically than his accomplishments as our chief executive officer. This could also be said of Washington, whose image has been a national symbol to millions who know nothing of what he did in his two terms of office, and certainly of Grant, whose military glory (one hopes) outshines the scandals of his administrations, and possibly of Kennedy, who offered a kind of spiritual rebirth to the nation that seems to be something apart from what he accomplished in his thousand days at the White House. Lincoln, of course, is the great example of the leader whose image and performance are of equally mammoth significance, though in his case the noble image, however like its original, was created largely after his assassination.

Alice Roosevelt Longworth, daughter of TR by his first marriage and survivor of all his offspring, remembered the father she loved with an admiration undimmed by sentimentality:

When I look back on it now, which I rarely do, I can feel a little mean about my father, especially as a politician rather than as a person. The eyebrows tend to lift and the canines to show. He was certainly right for the period he lived in. Absolutely perfect. It was a time when we needed large families and armies and expansion overseas. It was all in the great imperial tradition. But I tend to see it through the eyes of young people today, and one just can't have a prayerful attitude to it all.

It is true. What sounded right and inspiring to the cheering multitudes at the dawn of the twentieth century rings with a slightly tinny resonance today. And what survives in the panorama of history, even more than TR's trust-busting, or his building of the Panama Canal, or his negotiation of the Russo-Japanese War peace treaty, is the vision of the asthmatic youth who made a he-man of himself as a rancher in the Wild West, the intrepid Rough Rider who charged up San Juan Hill, the fearless antagonist of political vice and corruption, and the wielder of the "big stick" who sent his great white fleet around the globe to impress the alien powers with the spectacle of

America's might. There is almost no aspect of his life that is not relevant to some chapter of our history.

But to return to Alice Longworth's reservation. The following quotations should adequately demonstrate why much of our contemporary culture is at odds with TR's most treasured views. Here, to begin with, he writes on the respective functions of the sexes:

I believe that men and women should stand on an equality of right, but I do not believe that equality of right means equality of function, and I am more and more convinced that the great field, the indispensable field for the usefulness of woman, is the mother of the family. It is her work in the household, in the home, her work in bearing and rearing her children, which is more important than any man's work, and it is that work which should be normally the woman's work, just as normally the man's work should be that of the breadwinner, the supporter of the home, and if necessary the soldier who will fight for the home.

As a Harvard student he recorded in his diary: "Thank Heaven I am at least perfectly pure." Edmund Morris confirms this:

During his student years, nor indeed at any time in his life, did Theodore show the slightest tolerance for women, or for that matter men, who were anything but rigidly virtuous. . . . Sex to him was part of the mystical union of marriage, and, however pleasurable as an act of love, its function was to procreate. Outside marriage, as far as he was concerned, it simply did not exist.

Nor did he have anything but anathema for reluctant parents:

But the man or woman who deliberately avoids marriage and has a heart so cold as to know no passion and a brain so shallow and selfish as to dislike having children, is in effect a criminal against the race and should be an object of contemptuous abhorrence by all healthy people.

As to homosexuality, Alice Longworth, referring to a supposed remark made by Britain's George V: "I thought men like that shot themselves," commented, "My father was a bit like that."

Here is TR addressing the Naval War College on manly virtues:

All the great masterful races have been fighting races, and the minute that a race loses the hard fighting virtues, no matter what else it may retain, no matter how skilled in commerce and finance, in science or art, it has lost its right to stand as the equal of the best.

And the consequences of such a loss will be dire:

If we ever come to nothing as a nation, it will be because the teaching of Carl Schurz, President Eliot, the *Evening Sun*, and the futile sentimentalists of the international arbitration type bears its legitimate fruit in producing a flabby, timid type of character which eats away the great fighting features of our race.

When his own sons went to war he wrote:

I hope and pray that they'll all come back, but before God I'd rather none came back than one, able to go, had stayed at home.

In his autobiography he almost approves Britain's whipping of sex offenders:

There are brutes so low, so infamous, so degraded and bestial in their cruelty and brutality that the only way to get at them is through their skins.

And in the same book he took his stand on capital punishment:

But inasmuch as, without hesitation, in the performance of duty, I have again and again sent good and gallant and upright young men to die, it seems to me the height of folly both mischievous and mawkish to contend that criminals who have deserved death should nevertheless be allowed to shirk it.

Finally, there are many today who would deplore his emphasis on the savage cruelty of American Indians in *The Winning of the West* as perhaps a partial justification of the stringent treatment that we meted out to them.

The expression "too horrible to mention" is to be taken literally, not figuratively. It applies equally to the fate that has befallen every white man or woman who has fallen into the power of hostile Plains Indians during the last ten or fifteen years. The nature of the wild Indian has not changed. Not one man in a hundred, not a single woman, escapes torments which a civilized man cannot look another in the face and so much as speak of. Impalement on charred stakes, finger nails split off backwards, finger joints chewed off, eyes burnt out — these tortures can be mentioned, but there are others equally normal and customary which cannot even be hinted at, especially when women are the victims.

It should not be surprising, in view of the above and plenty of others, that there should have been critics who, according to Nathan Miller, have found TR "cunning, selfish, vindictive, melodramatic, megalomaniacal, dishonest, shallow, and cynical."

Such critics are far, however, very far, from giving us the true measure of the man. TR, it must always be borne in mind, had the lifelong habit of giving the freest reign to his tongue and pen, both publicly and privately, and it was his nature to be heartily emphatic, to make his points sometimes by gross overstatement. This by no means always reflected his true meaning, nor did it indicate that action would inevitably follow threat. He had wealths of reserve and was not above using bluster as a weapon. It is easy enough for a careful researcher to find justification for almost any interpretation of his acts in the 150,000 letters that he wrote or dictated, some running to many pages in length. But what the above quotations most certainly do not reveal is that their utterer was capable of the most profound political shrewdness, of a deep humanitarian concern, of a hatred of hypocrisy and deceit and a greatness of heart. TR was a political idealist who had the wisdom to know that only by astute and well-considered compromise in our legislative process could he hope to see enacted even a fraction of the social and military programs that he deemed — and in the opinion of this writer, correctly deemed — essential to the welfare of his nation. Which is why I believe he deserves his rank among our great presidents. He not only created an inspiring symbol — for his era, anyway — of courage and adventure in leadership; he contrived that his maneuvers "to get things done" should never descend from the strictly practical to the near corrupt. And we mustn't forget that in his day he could speak of standing at Armageddon to do battle for the Lord without being laughed off the platform.

One

The Roosevelts were an old Dutch family who immigrated to Manhattan in the seventeenth century and prospered there. In a photograph of Lincoln's New York funeral procession there can be seen the mansion of Cornelius Van Schaack Roosevelt, one of the city's ten millionaires with a fortune based in real estate and merchandising plate glass. Watching from one of the windows are two little boys, believed to be Cornelius's grandsons, Theodore Roosevelt Jr. and Elliott. Their father, Theodore Sr., lived more modestly in a brownstone on East Twentieth Street, where Theodore Jr., the future president, was born in 1858. He had been preceded by a sister, Anna, nicknamed Bamie, who in middle age married a naval officer, W. Sheffield Cowles, and was followed by another sister, Corinne, who wed the wealthy Douglas Robinson, and a younger brother, Elliott. The sisters, brilliant and admirable women, were lifelong devotees of their brother Theodore, but Elliott, despite good looks, charm, and intellectual ability, took early to drink and died a miserable failure, somewhat redeeming himself to history by fathering Eleanor.

Theodore Roosevelt Sr. had little inclination for business and devoted the time that his means afforded to substantial work in city charities and hospitals, attaining a wide reputation for good works. Theodore Jr. adored and worshiped him, but he also admitted that though his father had never once physically punished him, "he was the only man of whom I was ever really afraid." After the latter's premature death at forty-six he said: "I often feel badly that such a wonderful man as Father should have had a son of so little worth as I am."

Theodore Sr. had married a southern belle, Martha ("Mittie") Bulloch, from Georgia, who was lovely, gentle, self-indulgent, and something, one surmises, of a hypochondriac, who lay back on sofas and was waited on, hand and foot, by devoted family and servants. Her son Elliott called her "a sweet little Dresden monument." She had a brother, James Bulloch, of more vigorous character, the Confederate agent in Britain who masterminded the construction there, contrary to international law, of the commerce raider *Alabama,* which sank or captured fifty-seven Union merchant ships until at last it was sunk by the USS *Kearsage* off Cherbourg. Another brother of Mittie's, younger, a midshipman, Irvine, was rescued from the raider's wreck and was supposed to have fired its last shot.

I emphasize this because I think it had a strong effect on the whole life of young Theodore, or "Teedie," as he was known as a boy. Teedie's mother made no secret of her Confederate sympathies and was even (probably unreliably) credited with having draped the front of her house with the stars and bars after a Southern victory. But Teedie was fiercely Yankee and did not hesitate to pray aloud for the crushing of the Southern foe even in the presence of his beloved mother. How must he have felt when his hero father made the painful decision not to take up arms against his wife's compatriots and bought a substitute to fight for him? Oh, it was all very high-minded, and Theodore Sr. took up the complicated and unrewarded volunteer job of organizing a mailing system whereby servicemen could assign some of their pay to their often indigent families, but what was that to a boy who saw his maternal kin fighting for glory? Theodore Sr. came to regret his decision; according to Bamie he felt he should have put every other feeling aside to join the fighting forces. And Corinne believed that her brother's determination to make a military reputation was "in part compensation for an unspoken disappointment in his father's course in 1861."

I should put it even more strongly. The "unspoken" tells a tale. Theodore Jr. made a point of not mentioning the things that were most sacred to him. It is well known that he would never refer to his deceased first wife, even to their daughter, Alice. That he should not ever have discussed his father's course of action in a conflict as continually talked over in his day as the Civil War shows how deeply it must have penetrated. I have no doubt that he exonerated his father completely; saints could not be besmirched. But the saints' issue could be left with an ineluctable obligation to make up in the annals of military glory for the gap that the Roosevelts had suffered. Theodore Jr.'s throwing up of his assistant secretaryship of the navy in 1898 to become a Rough Rider when duty would have seemed to point to his staying at his post, his violent efforts as an ill and elderly man to get to the trenches in World War I, and his posting of his sons to battle all seem to stem from a barely rational compulsion. It is one thing for a father to salute his sons as they march off to fight for the right; it seems to me quite another to appeal, as he did, using all of his immense influence and prestige, to military authorities to speed them to the front. When his son Kermit thought he might get into action sooner by joining the British forces, his father did his best to pull strings to accomplish this, excusing himself to his friend Cecil Spring-Rice by saying that it was asking for a favor, "but the favor is that the boy shall have the chance to serve, and if necessary be killed in serving." And what is one to think of his attitude toward his son Archie, later to be severely wounded, when the latter asked for a few days' leave to be married before shipping to France and was accused of being a "slacker"? Or when he reproved his nephew-in-law, Franklin, assistant secretary of the navy and the father of five, for not chucking his job and enlisting? Had he, TR, not been in just that position in 1898? And was Franklin not by birth and marriage doubly a Roosevelt?

Teedie was an asthmatic child. His attacks could last for hours or days. He couldn't get enough air, gasping and choking and wheezing. When the attack was over, he would lie, sweat-soaked and trembling, dreading the next one. He was not sent to school except briefly to a local one; most of the time he was educated by tutors.

German, French, and some Italian were learned on two very extended European sojourns that the Roosevelts took in the decade that followed the Civil War. Teedie was absorbed in natural history, particularly at first in birds, and he became adept at taxonomy at an early age. He also, sometimes to the distress of the household, collected a private zoo of snakes, turtles, and mice.

When he was twelve his father called him in for a very serious talk that probably changed his life. "You have the mind but you have not the body, and without the help of the body the mind cannot go as far as it should. You must *make* your body!" The boy at once gave himself up to a strenuous course in calisthenics, the spirit of which he never again relaxed.

He developed his physique and with it a passion for the active outdoor life, which took him on expeditions to the wilderness where he cultivated the joy of hunting. By the time he entered Harvard he was sufficiently robust and full of a zest for life, with an income greater than the salary of Harvard's president, Charles W. Eliot. However, college presidents were not then well compensated, and many of the gilded youth of Boston and New York enjoyed greater allowances than young Theodore. But he did well enough for himself; he had his own rooms off campus and a horse and buggy with which to visit the beautiful Alice Lee, a Brahmin from Chesnut Hill, whom he had met early in his college career and whom he was already frantically determined to marry. He was also enthusiastic about his studies, asking so many questions in one class that the professor had to reprove him with a "I'm running this course, Mr. Roosevelt." And he eagerly cultivated the students of his own social background; it would take him a couple of years to shed his inherited snob-bishness, and we find him writing home that he stood nineteenth in his class, with only "one gentleman" ahead of him. But he was well enough liked, if considered a bit eccen-tric — his friend Robert Bacon would not visit his rooms because of the smell of his zoological specimens — and he was duly elected to the exclusive Porcellian Club. It is interesting to note that he chose for the topic of his senior essay "the practicability of equalizing men and women before the law," and that he didn't believe that in mar-riage a woman should assume her hus-band's name.

One thing he got off his mind at Harvard was all serious thought of a career in sci-ence. The emphasis was then all on laboratory work, and he was keen only for the out-of-doors. After graduation he married Alice Lee and settled down, following a honeymoon in Europe in which he abandoned his lovely bride long enough to scale the Matterhorn, to a New York life of mild law school and many social engagements. But that makes his life sound much less intense than it actually was. In the morning, yes, he attended law lectures at Columbia Law, not liking them very much but always attentive, and in the afternoon he moved to the public library, where he worked on a history of the War of 1812, which, however dry, has been continually praised and cited for the accuracy of its factual research. And if the evenings began with dinner parties they soon ran into competition with his new interest in Morton Hall, headquarters of the Twenty-first District Republican Association, whose meetings and discussions he began to attend, sometimes, to the amusement of the group, in evening dress, but always with a seriousness and dedication that they came to respect.

We do not know much about Alice's attitude toward this new interest of her husband's, but I think it safe to presume that it was a completely docile one. She is a slightly vague figure, an improbable partner for her dynamic spouse, but all seem to agree that she was sweet and agreeable — probably a bit dull. Anyway, he seems always to have adored her.

His fundamental interest in people was now bringing him closer to men of different backgrounds. He was also learning to appreciate the fact that social progress can only be accomplished by means that gentlemen of his sort had previously scorned. He was later to say: "I knew both the machine and the silk-stocking reformers fairly well. . . . The machine as such had no ideals at all, although many of the men composing it did have. On the other hand, the ideals of many of the silk-stocking reformers did not relate to the questions of real and vital interest to our people."

After two years of law school he gave it up to run as a Republican candidate for the Assembly in Albany and was elected for the year 1882, and thereafter reelected twice, for the years 1883 and 1884. His youth, his high, shrill voice, his aggressive desire to be heard, and his fancy clothes made him at first an object of curiosity and some ridicule, and it was felt even by some of his party that he was too violent in his denunciations of Democrats, but it didn't take him long to establish himself as a man to be heard. "I rose like a rocket," he later observed.

One of his early targets was a New York State judge, T. R. Westbrook, who corruptly aided Jay Gould in corruptly gaining control of the Manhattan Elevated Railway Company, going so far as actually to hold court in the offices of the speculators engaged in depressing the stock. TR went after him like a bulldog, distressing some of his associates who were inclined to use soft gloves in any sparring with such a power as Gould. But he obtained the judicial investigation he sought, and even though Westbrook was cleared he was publicly tarnished, and his subsequent death may well have been a suicide. TR, however, was not yet a notable liberal. Opposing a proposed ameliorization of conditions of virtual slavery in state prisons, he said he had "no maudlin sympathy . . . for men who had deliberately placed themselves outside the pale of society." In his final term in the Assembly he voted against a bill limiting the hours of streetcar conductors to twelve a day as a protection insulting to workers.

His trouble was that he still thought of a man, any man, as in total charge of his own destiny and therefore capable of choosing the terms of his employment and incurring total responsibility for his crimes. In the case of the legislature prohibiting the manufacture of cigars in homes, it would have been like the younger Roosevelt to have seen it as an invasion of basic rights, but when he became aware, through his own exhaustive investigations, of the sordid atmosphere that such a home industry created, he began to see that economic hardship could reduce men to near serfdom and that free will was possibly a monopoly of the well-to-do.

The crisis that changed his life now fell upon him. He and Alice had moved from a small brownstone to his widowed mother's mansion on West Fifty-seventh Street to await, in more comfortable circumstances, the birth of their first child. On February 14, 1884, Mittie Roosevelt died of typhoid and Alice of Bright's disease following the safe delivery of a daughter. "There is a curse on this house," Elliott told his desperate brother, arriving from Albany shortly before the double end. The latter recorded in his diary: "And when my heart's dearest died, the light went out from my life forever."

Two

TR had already invested a substantial percentage of his inherited capital in what turned out to be the ultimately losing proposition of a cattle ranch, Elk Horn, in the Badlands of the Dakota Territory, and now he resolved to conquer his sorrow in the new life this offered. Leaving his baby daughter Alice in the care of his still unmarried and willing sister Bamie, he became a rancher, rounding up his straying cattle for branding in the unfenced prairies, supervising his few employees while sharing all their tasks and taking long weeks off to hunt bison and grizzly bears in the wilderness. When he killed his first buffalo, according to his astonished guide Joe Ferris, he "broke into a wild facsimile of an Indian war dance."

He certainly proved himself the equal of the toughest cowboy. A drunken bully at a bar with two drawn pistols who called him "Four Eyes" because of his glasses was knocked out cold before he could raise a hand, and after the theft of some horses from his ranch TR and two of his men trailed the three thieves to their camp where they caught them with their rifles on the ground or on their shoulders. Creeping up on them, they covered them with cocked rifles and marched them for a solid week through the wilderness to a sheriff. At night during his watch over the culprits TR read *Anna Karenina*. It was true, as he once said, that "reading with me is a disease."

He had a simple formula for the conquest of fear. "There were all kinds of things of which I was afraid at first, ranging from grizzly bears to mean horses to gunfighters, but by acting as if I was not afraid, I gradually ceased to be afraid." And nothing soured the tremendous joy of living in the undeveloped West. He wrote: "There are few sensations I prefer to those of galloping over those rolling limitless prairies, rifle in hand, or winding my way among the barren fantastic and grimly picturesque deserts of the so-called Badlands."

Edmund Morris has summed up admirably what his western experience did for TR:

> During his time there he had built a massive body, repaired his soul, and learned to live on equal terms with men poorer and rougher than himself. He had broken horses with Hashknife Simpson,

joined in discordant choruses to the accompaniment of Fiddlin' Joe's violin, discussed homicidal techniques with Bat Masterson, shared greasy blankets with Modesty Carter, shown Bronco Charlie Miller how to "gentle" a horse, and told Hell-Roaring Bill Jones to shut his foul mouth.

In 1884 he returned to politics as a delegate to the Republican convention in Chicago where he initiated his lifelong friendship with Henry Cabot Lodge, a delegate from Massachusetts. Both men were strongly opposed, along with the liberal wing of their party, to the corrupt James G. Blaine, the leading contender, and unenthusiastic about the outgoing president, Chester A. Arthur, his principal rival. They backed Senator George Edmunds of Vermont, whose chances were small. Blaine was nominated, and the terrible question arose for the two new friends: would they stay with the party or desert it with the considerable number of high-minded liberals later to be known as mugwumps?

It was the great and deciding moment of TR's life. Would he cross the line to become a party man, a professional politician, or would he follow his ideals no matter what the cost to his own political future? When he became a delegate to the party's convention, had there not been an implied promise that he would support the man the convention chose? He decided anyway, and Lodge with him, that they would go along with Disraeli's famous growl: "Damn your principles! Stick to your party." And they were right, too. TR's career would have been ended had he bolted. He had been far too denunciatory of the Democrats for them ever to have advanced him, and, of course, the Republicans would never have trusted him again.

Both Lodge and TR had to suffer the scorn of some people they had previously admired, but TR's romantic view of the world enabled him in short order to see his role in the whole affair as a basically moral one and the mugwumps as hypocrites and traitors to the cause of right. His great gain was the lifelong (at least until the terrible crisis of 1912) support, advice, and devotion of the man soon to be a senator from Massachusetts. Lodge might have struck some as an odd contrast to TR. As Morris puts it: "Next to the wiry, bouncing, voluble Roosevelt, Lodge was tall, haughty, quiet, and dry. His beard was sharp, his coat tightly buttoned, his handshake quickly withdrawn." But both men were scholars of American history and lovers of horse riding and fox hunting; both combined an appreciation of the aristocratic standards for gentlemen with a relish for the rough-and-tumble of practical politics, and both were strong family men. TR said of Lodge: "From that time on he was my closest friend personally, politically, and in every other way, and occupied toward me a relation that no other man has occupied or will occupy."

In one of his multitudinous letters to Lodge he suggests one basis for their deep congeniality: "What funnily varied lives do we lead, Cabot! We touch two or three little worlds, each profoundly ignorant of the others. Our literary friends have but a vague knowledge of our actual political work, and a goodly number of our sporting and social acquaintances know us only as men of good family, one of whom rides hard to hounds while the other hunts big game in the Rockies."

As authors they read each other's books with relish. They were gentlemen historians in the path of Francis Parkman and William H. Prescott, determined that history, as a branch of literature, should be a work of the imagination as well as a compendium of facts. TR's most outstanding work is the four-volume *Winning of the West*. It may have been superseded, as most histories are, by works buttressed by later research, but it tells the basic story of the development of the continent in lively and readable chapters. The style breathes some of the spirit of the author:

From the Volga to the Pillars of Hercules, from Sicily to Britain, every land in turn bowed to the warlike prowess of the stalwart sons of Odin. Rome and Novgorod, the imperial city of Italy as well as the squalid capital of Muscovy, acknowledged the sway of the kings of Teutonic or Scandinavian blood.

One can see who had been raised on Gibbon and Macaulay! But TR's finest book, in the opinion of many, is his autobiography, which re-creates this strong man in strong prose so vivid that it has a value transcending its historical accuracy.

In 1886 TR ran for mayor of New York City and trailed the two leading contenders, Abram Hewitt, who was elected, and Henry George, who alarmed the voters as a socialist. Had TR won, would that have ended his political career as it has that of every other New York mayor to this date (2001)?

The great event, anyway, of the year was what followed shortly after his defeat: his marriage in London to Edith Carow.

A friend of his sister Corinne, she had known him since childhood and had always been supposed by the family to have been in love with him, even before the advent of Alice. She was certainly very different from Alice: firm of will, high-minded, intellectual, a lover of art and poetry, gracious but disciplined, a great lady but one who always regarded herself in the light of a loving support to a greater man. An adoring wife who allowed her spouse to absent himself in even the most difficult of domestic times for his long hunting trips (in 1910 one of ten months), she nonetheless did not hesitate to pull him up short when his exuberance took him over what she wisely deemed his limit. And she could be devastating, even a bit cruel, according to her stepdaughter, in her family reproaches. If his father was the only man of whom TR was ever afraid, Edith was perhaps the only woman. It is hard to see how he could have picked a better mate for his highly individual needs, or a better first lady for his ultimate home in the White House.

Despite his intense love for Edith, and his need of her — one mustn't forget his iron rules of chastity — he suffered deeply from his sense of guilt in betraying the memory of Alice. He wrote to his sister Bamie: "I utterly disbelieve in and disapprove of second marriages. I have always considered that they argued weakness in a man's character. You could not reproach me half as bitterly for my inconstancy and unfaithfulness as I reproach myself. Were I sure there was a heaven my prayer would be that I might never go there, lest I should meet those on earth who are dead."

Happily these feelings were overcome, and in the first dozen years of his second marriage he became, as he had always wanted to be, the explosively proud father of four sons and another daughter. Edith took over the care of young Alice from Bamie, so the family consisted of six. All four of his sons saw active service in World War I — the youngest fatally — and three in World War II, two dying in uniform.

The man who had held up the Republican standard in the New York mayoralty election and campaigned actively for President Benjamin Harrison in 1888 was owed something, and TR found himself appointed to the Civil Service Commission, where he served with a Democrat and a fellow Republican during the whole of the term of the not very helpful Harrison, whom he described as the "little gray man in the White House." He was reappointed by Grover Cleveland and served two more years before resigning to become one of New York City's four police commissioners.

TR made himself something of a pest to an administration largely intent on using civil service as a recompense for political support, but he did succeed in disgracing the Philadelphia store tycoon John Wanamaker, Harrison's postmaster general, before a congressional committee for failing to discipline twenty-five Baltimore postal employees for dunning their underlings to contribute to the Republican presidential campaign, and he did arrange, in his six years in office, to transfer twenty-six thousand jobs from the category of political plums to that of posts awarded on the basis of competitive examinations. Years later, as president, when he for once indulged his desire to encourage the arts by sneaking in a tiny job for the indigent poet Edwin Arlington Robinson, he chucklingly warned a correspondent: "Tell it not in civil service reform Gath, nor whisper it in the streets of merit-system Askelon."

But the great value to TR in these years was in getting to know official Washington and how it worked. He and Edith also developed a brilliant circle of friends there who enlivened their evenings with intellectual discussions and exchanges of wit: the Lodges, of course, and the John Hays and Henry Adamses. Adams found TR interesting but egocentric; he was amused but at times alarmed. He ascribed to him "that singular primitive quality that belongs to ultimate matter — the quality that medieval theology assigned to God — he was pure act." Hay, who was to become McKinley's secretary of state and hence TR's in 1901, enjoyed the latter's highest esteem, both as a statesman and the author of the great biography of Lincoln, but in later years TR somewhat altered this opinion, writing in 1909 to Lodge:

He was no administrator . . . he had a very easy loving nature . . . which made him shrink from all that was rough in life. . . . His intimacy with Henry James and Henry Adams — charming men but exceedingly undesirable companions for any man not of strong nature — and the tone of satirical cynicism which they admired and which he affected in writing them, marked that phase of his character which so impaired his usefulness as a public man.

41

On Henry James, who visited Henry Adams in Washington at this time, TR was harsh indeed. What he considered the latter's snobbish little tales about Yankees in Europe made him ashamed that James was an American. "Thus it is for the undersized man of letters, who flees his country because he, with his delicate effeminate sensitiveness, finds the conditions of life on this side of the water crude and raw, in other words, because he finds that he cannot play a man's part among men."

James in his correspondence gave as good as he got. He called TR "a dangerous and ominous jingo" and "the mere monstrous embodiment of unprecedented and resounding noise."

But at least some of the quality of those evenings of friendship is amusingly reflected in TR's later humorous inviting of himself to dinner at Mrs. (Nanny) Lodge's:

Then we could discuss the Hittite empire, the Pithecanthropus, and Magyar love songs and the exact relations of the Atli of the Volsunga Saga to the Etzel of the Nibelungenlied, and both to Attila — with interludes by Cabot about the rate bill.

Three

In 1895 TR accepted the post of president of New York City's Board of Police Commissioners, which he would hold for two years, and his family was able to move into the large country house that he had built in Oyster Bay for his first wife and which was to be the home he would always love. He had to have a residence in the city as well, for the job was very taxing — at least he soon made it so — and he gained an immediate public reputation for his lone checking on police beats at night, catching unwary officers asleep or in bars and curtly ordering them to their stations.

The job was made more difficult by the fact that there were three other commissioners who by no means always agreed with the policy of the president. But the greatest trouble that he had was caused by his decision to enforce the Sunday Excise Law, which forbade the sale of liquor on the Sabbath. The law had been supported by Tammany, which "protected" the saloons from police interference on Sunday in return for extracted coin. As the poorer elements of the city, notably the German and Irish neighborhoods, relied for a principal amusement on saloon drinking on their one day off, there was a general outcry against TR, rendered more bitter by the general knowledge that the rich could quaff all Sunday in their private clubs. But Roosevelt stuck to his guns, and in the end, despite the unpopularity gained in the city, his tough stand on enforcing a law with whose enactment he had had nothing to do, and with whose aim he had no particular sympathy, won him respect in the state.

In the fall of 1896 TR campaigned hard for William McKinley. The preceding decade had been marked by violent labor disturbances that had put much of the public in an antilabor mood: the Haymarket Square bombing in Chicago, the riots in the Homestead plant of the Carnegie Steel Company, the attempted assassination of Henry Clay Frick, and the Pullman strike. TR inveighed against agitators in his campaign speeches in a manner that must have satisfied the most conservative of his party. He said of the more radical advocates of the Democratic candidate, William Jennings Bryan, that they "have not the power to rival the deeds of Marat, Barrère, and Robespierre but that they are strikingly like the leaders of the Terror in France in mental and moral attitude."

How was he to be rewarded on McKinley's election? Senator Thomas Platt, the so-called easy boss of New York State politics and the undisputed master of the Republican machine there, had had some trouble with Roosevelt over his opposition to favoritism in the police department and opined that "he would probably do less damage to the organization as Assistant Secretary of the Navy than in any other office that could be named." But the president-elect was concerned with Roosevelt's reputation for hyperactivity. "I hope he has no preconceived plans that he would wish to drive through the moment he got in," he said. Lodge now intervened successfully, and McKinley was persuaded. Roosevelt became the assistant secretary under John Long, an easygoing gentleman with periods of ill health who was delighted to let his more forceful inferior handle most of the job.

It was the perfect one for TR. He had been a devoted student of the navy ever since his exhaustive work on the War of 1812, and he had hailed Admiral Mahan's *The Influence of Sea Power upon History, 1660–1783*, as the most important military document of the era. He flew to work to increase the number of our warships and make the existing ones more efficient, and his eyes must have gleamed as he saw in our deteriorating relations with Spain over Cuba the coming opportunity to prove our superiority at sea in both oceans by sinking the whole Spanish fleet.

As the crisis sharpened, and in one of Long's extended absences from Washington, TR took upon himself the responsibility of cabling Commodore George Dewey, the commander of the American Asiatic Squadron based in Japan: "Order the squadron . . . to Hong Kong. Keep full of coal. In the event of war with Spain your duty will be to see that the Spanish squadron does not leave the Asiatic coast."

TR justified such action in one of his letters saying: "He [Long] has wanted me to act entirely independently while he was away, and to decide all things myself, even where I had written him that I was going to decide them in a way that I doubted whether he would altogether like." The returning secretary, however, in this case was indignant at his junior's usurpation of authority, but war did come, and TR's instructions facilitated Dewey's dramatic victory in Manila Bay.

TR had already told the president that in

the event of war, he would resign his post and join the fighting forces, and no one could dissuade him from the resolution. Others may have doubted the culpability of Spain in the blowing up of the battleship *Maine*, visiting Havana on a peaceful mission, which triggered the American declaration of war; some doubt it even to this day, but no such reservations were harbored in the mind of the assistant secretary of the navy, who welcomed hostilities and wrote: "The *Maine* was sunk by an act of dirty treachery on the part of the Spaniards."

With the outbreak of war Congress authorized the formation of three regiments of volunteer cavalry to be raised among men in the Rockies and Great Plains who knew how to ride and shoot. The secretary of war offered TR a colonelcy and the command of one of these regiments, but he deemed his military qualifications inadequate. They consisted of three years in the National Guard in which he obtained a captaincy, and "not to speak of," as he put it, his having acted as "sheriff in the cow country." Of course, he could ride and shoot, but he thought it better to accept the rank of lieutenant colonel and serve under his friend, Colonel Leonard Wood, an army surgeon, but one who had a combat record and had been awarded the Medal of Honor in the campaign against the Apaches.

TR's new regiment, the First United States Cavalry, soon to be christened by the public as the "Rough Riders," was made up largely of men from New Mexico, Arizona, and Indian Territory, but it also included a goodly number of "dudes," socialite friends of TR from New York and Boston, passionate volunteers who had been adept at such sports as polo, fox hunting, and yachting. TR, however, was familiar with both sorts, and he knew how to unite them in a common goal and a common enthusiasm. Their training camp was in San Antonio, Texas.

TR was in primary charge of the field training while Colonel Wood took care of the difficult problems of requisition and supply. Edmund Morris has described the extent of Roosevelt's formidable task:

It would have taxed the powers of a Genghis Khan to place a thousand individualistic riders, accustomed to the freedom of polo, hunting, and the open range, upon a thousand half-broken horses, and then get them to advance, wheel, fan out, and divide in formation. Roosevelt's high-pitched orders led to bucking, biting, striking, and kicking. His first success was rewarded by an anonymous salute of six-shooter fire, causing a stampede into the San Antonio River.

And after all that, when the regiment arrived in Cuba, sailing from Tampa, Florida, for the attack on Santiago, it was to discover that they had no use for their horses, as the campaign was to be on foot! The Rough Riders, as one wag put it, had been converted into "Wood's Weary Walkers." Roosevelt, however, kept two horses, as he would have to move quickly from one position to another in leading and directing an advance. But his steed on San Juan Hill, if it made him more visible to his men, also made him more visible to the enemy, and he would cajole terrified men to follow him on the famous charge with the rasping cry: "Are you afraid to stand up when I am on horseback?"

None of the rough training in San Antonio was wasted in toughening and disciplining the men, and the regiment that landed in Cuba was forged into a cohesive and warlike unit that would help to win the war in a couple of months.

Those months, however, were not to be

easy ones. On their initial march through the jungle toward Santiago they encountered the enemy, drawn up on a ridge, at Las Guasimas. In the scrimmage that followed and lasted for two hours they found it hard to spot their foe, who was using smokeless powder while they had to make do with black powder whose smoke revealed their position. The Rough Riders had sixteen dead and fifty-two wounded, but they routed the enemy in the end and were able to continue their advance. TR distinguished himself by driving back the foremost flanks of the enemy and exposing the troops holding the ridge to the crossfire of the entire line of Rough Riders.

A reporter, Edward Marshall, observing TR in this action, wrote the following:

Perhaps a dozen of Roosevelt's men had passed into the thicket before he did. Then he stepped across the wire himself, and from that instant became the most magnificent soldier I have ever seen. It was as if that barbed wire strand had formed a dividing line in his life, and that when he stepped across it, he left behind in the bridle path all those unadmirable and conspicuous traits which have so often caused him to be justly criticized in civic life and found on the other side of it, in that Cuban thicket, the coolness and calm judgment and towering heroism which made him perhaps the most admired and best loved of all Americans in Cuba.

Edmund Morris is perhaps a bit hard on TR in assessing his reaction to the casualties at Las Guasimas, but as there is considerable evidence of a hard side in Roosevelt's nature I insert the following quotation to serve as a perhaps needed balance to the extreme praise in Marshall's opinion:

Compassion, never one of Theodore Roosevelt's outstanding characteristics, was notably absent from his written accounts of Las Guasimas and its aftermath — unless the perfunctory phrase "poor Capron and Ham Fish" can be counted to mean anything. His only recorded emotion as the Rough Riders buried seven of the dead the next morning, in a common grave darkened with the shadows of circling buzzards, was pride in its all-American variety: "Indian and cowboy, miner, packer and college athlete, the man of unknown ancestry from the lonely Western plains, and the man who carried on his watch the crest of the Stuyvesants and Fishes." When Bucky O'Neill turned to him and asked: "Colonel, isn't it Whitman who says of the vultures that 'they pluck the eyes of princes and tear the flesh of kings'?" Roosevelt answered coldly that he could not place the quotation.

The next objective of the invading Americans was San Juan Hill, crowned with a blockhouse that dominated the Camino Real leading to Santiago. Capture of the hill would mean possession of this main road over which the infantry and artillery could then proceed to the siege of Santiago. It was believed that the fall of Santiago would end the war, and so it proved.

Fever in the high command led to some last-minute promotions, and the elevation of Wood raised TR, to his great satisfaction — for now he deemed himself fully qualified — to the command of the Rough Riders. But the Rough Riders were not the only troops now waiting impatiently at the bottom of the hill for the order to charge and suffering from the withering and well-aimed fire of the defenders above them. There were also officers superior to TR, and he was frantic with the notion that the glory of leading the charge might be denied him. At last a message was received: "Move forward and support the Regulars in the assault on the hills in front." This was not a total license, but it was all TR needed: "The instant I received the order I sprang on my horse, and then my 'crowded hour' began."

His men followed him up the hill, and victory was achieved. "All men who feel any power in battle," he wrote, "know what it is like when the wolf rises in his heart." And Richard Harding Davis, who watched the great charge, said of it: "No man who saw Roosevelt take that ride expected he would finish it alive."

And America had a new hero, as John Morton Blum has put it: "Between the war with Spain and the war in Europe, the average American boy, discarding the log cabin and the split rail, adopted a new model of successful conduct — a model that his father, however he voted, cheered throatily, and his mother, however she worshipped, endorsed."

Of course, there was another side, the other side of war. Roosevelt shot a Spaniard only ten yards away; he bowled over "like a jack rabbit." And after the heights were taken he exulted to an old friend and fellow trooper, Robert Ferguson, "Look at all those damned Spanish dead!" Ferguson wrote to Edith Roosevelt: "No hunting trip so far has ever equalled it in Theodore's eyes. It makes up for the omissions of many past years . . . T was just reveling in victory and gore."

Now came the big job of getting the boys home before half of them died of malaria. General Shafter called a conference of all brigade and division commanders to discuss the inexcusable delays of the government in arranging fast transportation for the victorious troops. A communication had to be addressed to the War Department, but the regulars naturally feared the injury to their careers involved in angering Secretary Russell Alger or President McKinley himself. It was Roosevelt, of course, who took the matter in hand and drafted a round-robin letter to be signed by all present and sent to the Associated Press:

> We, the undersigned officers . . . are of the unanimous opinion that this Army should at once be taken out of the Island of Cuba and sent to some point on the Northern seacoast of the United States . . . that the army is disabled by malarial fever to the extent that its efficiency is destroyed, and that it is in a condition to

be practically entirely destroyed by an epidemic of yellow fever which is sure to come in the near future. . . . This army must be moved at once or perish. As the army can be safely moved now, the persons responsible for preventing such a move will be responsible for the unnecessary loss of many thousands of lives.

The secretary of war was outraged; so was the president; there was talk of a court-martial for Roosevelt, but within three days Shafter's army was ordered to Montauk, Long Island. No one really cared to take on the hero of San Juan Hill.

But of course there had to be jokes. Finley Peter Dunne, "Mr. Dooley," spoofing Roosevelt's published account of the war in a piece entitled "Alone in Cuba," rephrased the boast of the author, now a candidate for the governorship of New York, that he had killed a Spaniard with his pistol: "I fired at th' man nearest to me an' I knew by th' expression iv his face that th' trusty bullet wint home. It passed through his frame, he fell, an' wan little home in far-off Catalonia was made happy be th' thought that their riprisintitive had been kilt be th' future governor of New York." One is glad to learn that TR was amused by this and actually told Dunne so.

Roosevelt maintained a constant correspondence with Lodge, even from the front lines, and used the senator to bring his complaints on military incompetence to the attention of the government. He was not temperate in his language. "Not since the campaign of Crassus against the Parthians has there been so criminally incompetent a general as Shafter, and not since the expedition against Walcheron has there been grosser mismanagement than in this."

He urged Lodge to see that he be awarded the Medal of Honor. "I don't ask this as a favor; I ask it as a right. . . . If I didn't earn it, then no commissioned officer ever can earn it." But his complaints had been too harsh and too public; the army brass could never forgive, and he never received the coveted medal. Regular service officers have long memories, and the refusal of President Wilson, two decades later, to allow him to form a regiment to take to France, strongly supported by the army chiefs, may have contained an element of this old resentment.

On January 16, 2001, Congress did award the medal posthumously to TR.

Four

TR's wartime popularity almost required the New York Republicans to run him as candidate for the governorship, as they had no other candidate so likely to win. But Thomas Platt, the "easy boss," would rather have lost the election than gain a chief executive who would loosen his iron grip on the party. Holding forth in his usual corner of the lobby of a Manhattan hotel, he met with Roosevelt to hash out the terms under which he and the ebullient colonel might agree to operate the state. The two men could not have been more different: Platt, dry, concentrated, essentially humorless, the quintessential machine politician, by no means indifferent to the welfare of his constituents but resolutely determined that he and his selected men, and only they, should be in well-compensated charge of such welfare; and Roosevelt, the all-curious, the man of so many interests that he was called a polygon. With his gift for portraiture TR described his partner-opponent: "He lived in hotels and had few extravagant tastes. Indeed, I could not find that he had any tastes at all, except on rare occasions for a dry theology wholly divorced from moral implications." One of Roosevelt's most painful concessions to this tasteless hotel resident was withdrawing his support for his friend Joseph H. Choate, who was running against Platt for a Senate seat.

Platt and he came at last to an understanding under which, in return for the nomination, TR would consult with him on all political appointments, and Roosevelt was duly elected. Reformers were dismayed by such dealings, which they could not believe were not made at the cost of essential decencies, but TR perfectly understood that a failure to deal with the machine would mean a failure to make any social progress at all, and he adopted the course of compromise quite openly. He never made any secret of his regular breakfasts with Platt during his two-year term, and he described in his autobiography how, when it was necessary on important issues to go against Platt, it behooved him to conduct himself:

My aim was to make a fight only when I could so manage it that there could be no question in the minds of honest men that my prime purpose was not to attack Mr. Platt or anyone else, except as a necessary incident to securing clean and efficient government.

Later, as president, TR would speak of his shuddering "when I read Senator Platt's testimony today in which he said that he recognized it as a moral obligation to take care of the interests of the corporations that contributed to the campaigns." And when the aging Platt was challenged for leadership of the New York political machine by the equally unscrupulous Governor Benjamin Odell, TR likened the former to old Akela, the leader of the wolf pack in Kipling's *Jungle Book*, who "has lost his teeth and his spring" but must still be harried to death in battle by his would-be successor. "I get fairly heartsick in the effort to avoid quarreling with them," TR wrote, "and yet do my duty as a clean and decent man."

What threatened to be a major embarrassment in TR's campaign for the governorship was the fact that he had given his residence on certain tax forms as the District of Columbia, but Elihu Root cleared this up, and all was well. TR's short governorship was characterized by his improvement of the organization of the canal system, the state's corrective institutions, and the factory inspector's office, but his real victory lay in inducing the legislature to pass an act taxing the franchises of public utilities. This was a significant step in what came to be his lifelong policy of restraining the too ample power of the great business corporations and resulted in a fight with Platt so vigorous that the easy boss, despite a certain curious respect and even fondness for his troublesome opponent, decided that the best way to get rid of him was once again to send him down to Washington. That Roosevelt was entirely aware of this is made clear by this letter to Lodge:

I have found out one reason why Senator Platt wants me nominated for the Vice-Presidency. He is, I am convinced, genuinely friendly, and indeed I think I may say, really fond of me, and is personally satisfied with the way I have conducted politics; but the big money men with whom he is in close touch and whose campaign contributions have certainly been no inconsiderable factor in his strength, have been pressing him very strongly to get me put in the Vice-Presidency so as to get me out of the state.

He regarded the proposed office as honorable but as one in which there was not much to do; he would be "planted" for four years. He would have much preferred the governor-generalship of the Philippines. But Lodge, who saw himself, and with every justification, as the guardian of his friend's career, insisted that the vice presidency was the right next step, and Roosevelt was nominated, elected, and rendered twenty-sixth president of the United States by the bullet of Leon Czolgosz on September 14, 1901.

William McKinley, in his first term and in his brief interrupted second, had been a conservative president, the choice and favorite of large industrial and financial interests, and his successor by no means shared this esteem. Indeed, the right wing of the Republicans had conspired to get rid of him, and now, as Mark Hanna wailed: "Look what we've got! That damned cowboy is president of the United States!" Certainly, they saw Roosevelt as a threat, but it is not clear that they saw him as a progressive, or what they would have termed a socialist, threat. It is more likely that they saw him, as in Hanna's eyes, as an irresponsible and unpredictable cowboy with a wild record of persecuting businesses for minor infractions of the law and a distressing tendency to call for taxes on corporations.

Just when in his career, then, did TR gain his reputation as a social reformer? None of his three closest friends and advisers, Lodge, Root, or William Howard Taft, were noted liberals.

Elihu Root, who until their breakup in 1912 was the most respected of the three by TR, though Lodge was always the most intimate, was a witty sardonic man who was never afraid to puncture any man's bubble, including Roosevelt's, with a lethally aimed barb. A brilliant Wall Street corporation lawyer and a stalwart of the Republican Party, he had first come to TR's close attention when he was retained to straighten out the near scandal aroused in the gubernatorial campaign by the discovery that Roosevelt had given his residence as the District of Columbia in a tax return. Edmund Morris has described Root's method of work so well that I quote it in full:

Root set to work on Roosevelt's affidavits and correspondence. Analysis of the latter showed that the candidate was more sinned against than sinning; he had received foolish advice from family lawyers and accountants, despite repeated pleas to them to protect his voting rights. But the cold evidence was embarrassing.

Roosevelt had definitely declared himself the resident of another state during the required period of eligibility. Root decided to prepare a brief on varying interpretations of the word *resident,* mixing many "dry details" with sympathetic extracts from Roosevelt's letters, plus a lot of patriotic "ballyhoo" calculated both to obfuscate and inspire.

It is not hard to imagine what TR may have suffered from Root's sarcastic remarks as he explained this brief to his client, but he was always to take Root's cracks with commendable equanimity, realizing that his candor was an integral part of his sagacity. And Root's devotion to and admiration of Roosevelt was strong and constant. Even Edith, who did not like Root because he had once expressed satisfaction that her husband had damaged an arm on one of his overly athletic excursions around Washington, agreed that he was a valuable adviser, in that nothing deterred him from speaking his mind.

Root, as the counsel for giant business interests, was hardly a liberal cabinet member in either of the offices he held, War and State, but he was a sane and solid administrator, later an able senator, and he was awarded a Nobel Peace Prize. Nor was Lodge anything like a radical, though his respect for an earlier and more ethical and gentlemanly generation of Boston merchants, including his own forebears, had engendered a certain lofty scorn for the cruder new rich of his day. And Taft, who seemed to have proved himself a staunch supporter of Roosevelt's Square Deal, was to veer to the right when he found himself at the helm.

Roosevelt, prior to his presidency, had shown no extraordinary concern either for labor or for the disadvantaged. He cared about them as all decent persons cared, but they were not among his primary concerns. A deeply moral man, he was first and foremost taken up in a lifelong and enthusiastic fight against lawbreakers; he was a policeman at heart, which was obviously why he had done so well as a commissioner in New York. And above all, he detested bullies: the foulmouthed gunmen he had seen terrifying customers in western bars, the backroom machine politicians who milked the urban poor, the Pennsylvania mining tycoons who exploited their ignorant immigrant laborers. Like a Byronic hero he wanted not so much to raise the poor as to lower the proud.

But such can be a fertile soil for the growth of a wider compassion, and this is what happened to him in the Washington years.

Five

"It's a dreadful thing to come into the presidency this way," TR wrote, "but it would be a far worse thing to be morbid about it." And morbid was something he never was. But soon, despite the care that the Roosevelts took to do nothing that would jar the national mourning, an air of busy exuberance began to emanate from the White House and steal across the country. Lincoln Steffens offered this glimpse of the forty-two-year-old president:

> His offices were crowded with people, mostly reformers, all day long, and the President did his work among them with little privacy and much rejoicing. He strode triumphant around among us, talking and shaking hands, dictating and signing letters and laughing. Washington, and the whole country, was in mourning, and no doubt the President felt he should hold himself down; he didn't, he tried to, but his joy showed in every word and movement.

Edith Roosevelt, who busied herself removing the tasseled remnants of late-Victorian bad taste and restoring the White House interior to something more like its classical simplicity and dignity, presided with quiet grace over the evening festivities, always insisting that the public had no right to interviews with the first lady, and that all such attention should be focused on the president himself. But even she found it difficult to shield her noisy and active brood from the loving attention of the crowd. Her stepdaughter, beautiful and decidedly independent, was known to an admiring press as "Princess Alice," and the boys were an integral part of the White House vision as it appeared to every visitor. A crowd waiting outside the gate was once astonished to see the departing president making grotesque faces out the window of his carriage, not realizing that he was continuing some game with little Quentin waving from the doorstep.

TR was a devoted father and never missed some sort of romp with his offspring every evening, even on the busiest day. He adored them and they him, but this was never at the expense of any homework or discipline, and the whole family, with enacted gravity, could lend itself to a deserved punishment, as shown in this charming excerpt from one of TR's letters:

Last night I had to spank Quentin for taking something that didn't belong to him and then not telling the truth about it. Ethel and Mother acted respectively as accuser and court of first resort, and then brought him solemnly into me for sentence and punishment — both retiring much agitated when the final catastrophe became imminent. Today Quentin has become as cunning as possible. He quite understood that he had brought his fate on himself.

TR needed a good deal of physical exercise, particularly to control a waistline responding to his hearty meals. He played tennis with aides, but he preferred riding and long hikes. On one of the latter, accompanied by some more or less willing diplomats, he encountered a stream that could be forded only by the removal of all clothing. J. J. Jusserand, the French ambassador and TR's good friend, emulated his host except for a pair of pink gloves. Asked why he retained these, he replied: "In case we should run into ladies."

More serious was TR's passion for boxing, and his habit of sparring with younger and stronger men. He finally abandoned it after a young artillery captain smashed enough blood vessels in his left eye to cause permanent dimness. Ultimately, indeed, he lost all sight in that eye. He had the consideration to make sure that the officer's name was never made public.

Such an incident must have warned even an enthusiast like TR of the dangers of too great an emphasis on physical energy, for we find him writing to his German friend, Hermann von Sternberg, that if it was an excellent thing for him to go on a lion hunt or to ride a blooded hunter, "it would be a very bad thing indeed if I treated either exercise as anything but a diversion and as a means of refreshing me for doing double work in serious government business." And at another time we see him reminding his son Teddie that athletic proficiency is a good servant but a bad master, and that Pliny had advised Trajan to keep the Greeks absorbed in athletics to distract their minds and prevent their ever being dangerous to the Romans.

No president, surely, could have worked harder at the job than TR, yet he was possessed with such a ranging curiosity that he wondered at times if he was giving the myriad political questions that came before him the entire absorption he supposed they deserved. "I do not regard them as being one-tenth or one-hundredth part as important as so many other questions in our life," he once observed. And at another time: "I have had a most vivid realization of what it must have meant to Abraham Lincoln, in the midst of the heartbreaking anxieties of the Civil War, to have to take up his time in trying to satisfy the candidates for postmaster in Chicago." Yet, even dealing with the problems inherent under a free representative government, particularly in foreign relations, he reminded himself that it was "rather a comfort to feel that Russia, where freedom has been completely sacrificed, where the darkest and most reactionary tyranny reigns, has as yet been unable to do well in the exercise of these functions."

Always, in his work, he needed the constant distraction and stimulation of reading. He wrote to his friend, the British historian George Trevelyan: "To succeed in getting measures like these through [Congress] one has to be a rough-and-tumble man oneself, and I find it a great comfort to like all kinds of books, and to get half an hour or an hour's complete rest and complete detachment from the fighting of the moment by plunging into the genius and misdeeds of Marlborough . . . or in short anything that Macaulay wrote . . . or any one of most of the novels of Scott, or some of the novels of Thackeray and Dickens."

Which brings us to those "measures" that he had to get through Congress. It is common in our time to regard the president as initiating not only legislation but a whole coordinated program of it. But it is well to remember that TR was considered unusual in his day for undertaking to alter the philosophy of government in its relation to the vast business enterprises that regarded themselves arrogantly as the true guardians of the American dream. What he accomplished in the seven years of his two terms seems small enough in contrast to the sweeping control exercised by Washington ever since the advent of the New Deal in 1933, but his importance is that of a pioneer. In his day he started a healthy discord between the "irresponsible demagogue," as the tycoons called him, and the "malefactors of great wealth," as he called *them*.

To sum up the major legislative accomplishments of Roosevelt in his two terms of office one might list them as follows: the Elkins Law, against the railroads' practice of giving rebates to favored customers; the creation of the Department of Commerce and Labor with its Bureau of Corporations, which grew to regulate every business that crossed state lines; the Hepburn Bill, which amended and vitalized the Interstate Commerce Act and gave government the power to set railroad rates; the Pure Food and Meat Inspection Laws, which remedied some of the scandals of the meatpacking industry as exposed by Upton Sinclair's novel *The Jungle*; and the Employers' Liability and Safety Appliance Laws, which limited the hours of employees.

The first national crisis, however, that the new president had to handle called not for legislation but for executive action, or at least the threat of such, and at a time, too, when the constitutional authority for any such action was far from clear. In 1902 the United Mine Workers under the leadership of John Mitchell called a strike that shut down the anthracite coal mines. Coal prices quadrupled from five dollars a ton to twenty, and mobs anticipating freezing weather began to stop coal-carrying freight trains to steal their cargo. The operators rigidly refused any concession to the strikers, and the country was threatened with a devastating winter. TR did not know what action was available to him; he finally adopted the neutral course of inviting both sides to come to the capital to discuss the issues with him.

The operators were intransigent and even ill-mannered. Their principal spokesman, George F. Baer, president of the Philadelphia and Reading Coal & Iron Company, expressed his economic philosophy as follows: "The rights and interests of the laboring man will be protected and cared for — not by the labor agitators but by the Christian men to whom God in his infinite wisdom has given the control of the property interests of this country." TR found Mitchell, the union leader, "the only one who kept his temper and his head." Perhaps the president understood the enthusiasm of the miners who sang the spirited ballad ending: "So shtrike can come, like son of a gun, me Johnny Mitchell man!" Baer would have simply pointed out that the song justified his saying of the workers: "They don't suffer; they can't even speak English!"

Roosevelt appealed to his lawyers and wondered whether he didn't have the power under common law, if not under the Constitution, to take over the management of the coal companies on the principle that any peasant has the right to take wood that is not his if necessary for the preservation of life in winter weather. Root thought so, anyway. At last TR bit the bullet and announced that if an accord was not reached federal troops would take over the mines and run them as a receivership.

At this, the operators agreed to binding arbitration by an impartial board to consist of a mining engineer, an army engineer, a businessman, a federal judge, and an eminent sociologist. But the union insisted on a union man, which the operators stoutly resisted until Roosevelt broke the impasse by suggesting a union man who was also an eminent sociologist! The strike ended, and the arbitrators gave the workers a nine-hour day and a 10 percent wage raise. No recognition, however, was accorded the union.

Six

TR soon gained a reputation as a radical among the major financiers and business moguls of his day. So fervently held was this notion that a part of it stuck to him. Decades later, in New Deal days, the now veteran Endicott Peabody, headmaster of Groton School to which TR had sent his boys, read aloud to a group of right-wing graduates a letter from another graduate denouncing "Roosevelt" for every crime in the book. His audience, assuming that the reference was to FDR, their bête noire though a fellow alumnus, warmly applauded. "But wait!" the chuckling headmaster cautioned them. "This letter was written in 1905!" In fact, TR, like his distant cousin and nephew-in-law, was neither by birth, upbringing, nor mature inclination in the least bit a radical.

He had no hostility as such to big business, and certainly no feeling of guilt about inherited wealth, including his own. And his early attitude toward labor was very much that of his class; he adhered to the classic credo that every man is master of his fate, and he viewed with suspicion the claims of unions to speak for all employees including dissenters and nonunion men. But his anger against exploitation, when it was revealed to him, was dire, and what was a greater exploiter in his day than a company in the grip of such a man as Jay Gould? It was not the power of business enterprise that bothered him, but what he saw as its criminal misuse.

With TR the crux of almost every great decision was a moral one. He once wrote to a friend pressing him for further reforms:

> While I agree with you that energetic, and, in the long run radical, action must be taken to do away with the effects of arrogant and selfish greed on the part of the capitalist, yet I am more than ever convinced that the real factor in the elevation of any man or any mass of men must be the development within his or their hearts of the qualities which alone can make even the individual, the class, or the nation permanently useful to themselves and to others.

That is hardly the sentiment of a Marx or a Lenin.

There always had to be an element of wrongdoing in anything TR sought to crush, a touch of crusade in any such proceeding. To him there were good trusts and bad trusts. Bad trusts sought to profit by restricting production by trick or device, by plotting against competitors, by oppressing wage earners, or by extorting high prices for a commodity made artificially scarce. If bad trusts were not disciplined and regulated, then the real radicals would take over. As he put it: "We seek to defy law-defying wealth, in the first place to prevent its doing evil, and in the next place to avoid the vindictive and dreadful radicalism which if left uncontrolled it is certain in the end to arouse." In similar fashion some of the advocates of the New Deal would later claim that FDR had saved the nation from revolution.

The Northern Securities case was TR's first major move against the trusts. Capitalized at four hundred million dollars and dominated by J. P. Morgan, Northern Securities was the holding company for the controlling stock of James J. Hill's Northern Pacific Railway and of E. H. Harriman's Union Pacific, thus preempting most of the rails of the American Northwest. Hill, Harriman, and Morgan had dreamed of transcontinental lines that would link the industrial centers of the United States with the markets of the East and had been assured by counsel that the Sherman Antitrust Act was aimed against restraint of trade and not restraint of competition. It was also reassuring to them that the act had not previously been much of a threat to big business and had indeed been more frequently invoked against labor unions. And there was indeed a good deal to be said for railroad mergers, though to small farmers and businessmen it seemed that such near monopolies juggled the stock market and overcharged for freight. TR may have echoed their sentiment when he said: "Of all forms of tyranny the least attractive and the most vulgar is the tyranny of mere wealth."

He instructed his attorney general, Philander Knox, to prosecute Northern Securities and its directors as a combination in restraint of trade. He did not consult his cabinet, and the shock of his attack brought the outraged Morgan in protest to the White House. If there was anything wrong, he demanded of the president, why had he not sent "his man" to consult with "my man" to fix it up? But TR did not want to fix it up; he wanted to break it up. Morgan's attitude — that the government of the United States was merely another corporate entity on equal terms (at the most) with the Morgan bank — confirmed TR in his attitude that he had embarked on the right course.

The Supreme Court ultimately upheld the government's position, but only five to four. Still, that was enough to put permanent teeth in the ineptly drawn Sherman Act, which was thereafter wielded with considerable effect against some of the nation's major trusts. But Oliver Wendell Holmes Jr., newly appointed to the court by TR on the strong recommendation of his friend Lodge, dissented. He argued that the Sherman Act applied only to combinations that had been illegal in common law, such as agreements between X company and Y company that Y will never engage in X's business, and that the Act said nothing about preserving competition and nothing about a necessary connection between size and monopoly status. Under the majority's opinion, he pointed out, two small stagecoach companies, operating across state lines, could be prosecuted if they merged.

Holmes recognized, however, that more had been expected of the Sherman Act, both by the public and possibly even by its framers:

There is a natural feeling that somehow or other the statute meant to strike at combinations great enough to cause great anxiety on the part of those who love their country more than their money, while it viewed such little ones as I have supposed with just indifference. This notion, it may be said, breathes from the pores of the Act, though it seems to be contradicted in every way by the words in detail.

Holmes did not think it was the function of the judiciary to rewrite even a badly drafted law to the extent that would have been required here, and I agree with him. The president did not; he was outraged. He had expected any judge he appointed to do his best to carry out the spirit of the law as interpreted by the party in power, and if five good judges could see fit to stretch the statute to accord with the probable intent of the clumsy framers, who was Holmes to quibble over a few phrases? "I could carve a better judge out of a banana," he snorted. This was not TR at his best.

Holmes shrugged off the White House's reaction and repeated to friends a quip supposedly made by a senator: "What the boys like about Roosevelt is that he doesn't give a damn about the law!" But his final verdict on TR, given years later, was graver. Writing to his friend, Sir Frederick Pollock, and recalling that Roosevelt couldn't forgive anyone who stood in his way, he added: "He was very likeable, a big figure, a rather ordinary intellect, with extraordinary gifts, a shrewd and I think rather unscrupulous politician. He played all his cards — if not more."

TR may have indeed been petty on the subject of Holmes's dissent, but his attitude toward constitutional law was that of any progressive chief executive whose primary concern was to see legislation judicially interpreted in ways to foster his social programs. He had no desire to subvert the Constitution; he simply wanted it to operate for what he considered the good of the nation as a whole and not for the benefit of any particular social or commercial class. He was always irate, for example, at the nullification of the Constitution by the action of southern states in virtually disenfranchising the Negro, but he had been helpless to correct it in view of the solidity of his opponents and the then indifference of the North. He had been also angered by the conversion of the Fourteenth Amendment into a charter of liberty for the great corporations, but here he was by no means helpless, as the Northern Securities case had shown.

He had never been much drawn to the study of law. Even in his brief time at law school he had been repelled by the doctrine of caveat emptor, which flew in the teeth of what to him was the revered code of a gentleman's honor. How could any man calling himself that invoke a law to protect himself from some poor bloke to whom he had sold shoddy goods? TR was always more of a humanitarian than Holmes, who tended to look rather askance at the common herd of mankind and who defined freedom of speech, despite his resolution to protect it, as "the right of a fool to drool." Roosevelt always insisted that he had never usurped power, that he had simply used it, whenever he could get his executive hands on it, and as broadly as possible, for the benefit and protection of the nation placed in his charge.

When TR observed to a friend that he always wanted a great constitutional lawyer at his side, and the friend pointed out that he had always had the services of William Howard Taft and Elihu Root, both undisputed authorities in the field, he retorted: "Yes, but they don't always agree with me."

Seven

In 1901, when TR took office, the Isthmus of Panama was legally, however tenuously, a part of the Republic of Colombia. In the preceding half century more than fifty riots and attempted uprisings had signaled the perennial discontent of the Panamanian people in their frustrated desire for independence. Many of these had been put down by the Colombian government with the military assistance of the United States. Rusting in the jungles of the isthmus was the rotting machinery of the French company that had failed in its attempt to build a transoceanic canal, but which still held the Colombian concession for such a waterway. Obviously the company desperately hoped to sell this concession to the American government for forty million dollars (less than half its original asking price). Its representative in these negotiations was a very clever and wily Frenchman living in Panama, Philippe Bunau Varilla, ably aided by his New York counsel, William Nelson Cromwell. Both men well understood the ambitious and aggressive nature of the American president and knew how to dangle in front of him the lure of a waterway that would change the navigation of the seas and double the striking power of our navy.

The legal position of the United States, in the event of its failure to obtain Colombia's consent to operate under the purchased French concession, was hazy, to say the least. A treaty between Colombia (then New Granada) and the United States in 1846 guaranteed the United States the right of transit across the isthmus, but there was some question whether Colombia was bound by a treaty made by New Granada, its predecessor state, even though TR clung to the theory suggested by a lawyer that the treaty was similar to a covenant running with the land. The proposed Hay-Pauncefort Treaty in 1898 between Britain and the United States would have given the two signatories a partnership in any canal to be constructed and would have prohibited its military defense, but TR had seen that it would be contrary to his basic naval needs to open the canal to possible enemies and also wanted sole control, both of which points were conceded in the second treaty. Congress was willing now to go along with the canal project; the Nicaraguan route was abandoned; Cromwell's deal with the

French was accepted — everything was ready. Colombia was offered ten million dollars outright and a quarter of a million a year for rent, when suddenly Bogotá changed its mind and demanded much more.

What happened now was that patience ran out. There was a feeling in our administration that the Colombian government was hopelessly corrupt and impossible to deal with. Bunau Varilla and Cromwell had their revolution ready in Panama; all they needed was help from the United States in blocking the landing of any Colombian troops sent to quell the rebellion. Was that not part of the long-accepted role of Uncle Sam in preserving order in the isthmus? Anyway, the landings were blocked, and with the loss of only one life, an innocent bystander. The Republic of Panama was promptly recognized and promptly established, and the way was clear for American engineers to start their huge and totally successful project of uniting the two oceans.

TR would again and again seek to justify his role in the whole business, not always to everybody's satisfaction. At the outset he wrote to his son Kermit: "Any interference that I undertake now will be in the interest of the United States and of the people of the

Panama Isthmus themselves. There will be some lively times in carrying out this policy." In 1911 he stated: "While I was president I kept my foot down on these revolutions [the sporadic Panamanian riots], so that when the revolution referred to did occur, I simply lifted my foot." And in the usual fashion of his defense he lambasted the Colombians morally: "Panama revolted from Colombia because Colombia, for corrupt and evil purposes, or else from complete governmental incompetency, declined to permit the building of the great work which meant everything to Panama. By every law, human and divine, Panama was right in her position." His action, he asserted, was only opposed by "a small body of shrill eunuchs who consistently oppose the action of this government whenever that action is to its own interests. Even though at the same time it may be immensely to the interest of the world." His final blast was this: "To the worst characteristics of seventeenth-century Spain, and of Spain at its worst under Philip II, Colombia has added a squalid savagery of its own, and it has combined with exquisite nicety the worst forms of despotism and of anarchy, of violence and of fatuous weakness, of dismal ignorance, cruelty, treachery, greed, and utter vanity."

Yet again in the year 1911, speaking in Berkeley, California, he made what some critics have deemed the ultimate confession. Referring to his having recognized the new government of Panama without waiting for Congress to be in session, he stated: "I took the Canal Zone and let Congress debate."

Perhaps Elihu Root, his brilliant secretary of war at the time, had the last word at a cabinet meeting in which TR undertook to explain just what he had done and why. Root, whose dry wit and acidity were appreciated by a chief who, despite his strong opinions, understood the importance of candor in his staff and could even laugh at it, concluded that before hearing the president's defense he had deemed him guilty only of seduction but he now saw him guilty of rape!

One of the several things that TR never forgave Woodrow Wilson for was the latter's action as president in apologizing to Colombia for our role in acquiring the Canal Zone and in persuading Congress to make a compensating grant.

How do we think of TR's action today? Should he have waited for further negotiations with Colombia? But even had Colombia agreed on a price for the concession, would it have been feasible to construct the canal in the teeth of Panamanian intransigence? Might they not have seen the waterway as enhancing their tyrant's power and prestige and sought to sabotage the work? TR saw his chance to improve world trade and render our fleet more formidable against an already menacing Japan at the price of giving independence to a small oppressed nation that passionately desired its liberty. And all at the price of a single life! When one thinks of what the United States has done in our time all over the globe to foment resistance to dictators, sometimes at a questionable gain either to us or to the people we aimed to help, it seems to me that one must think twice before calling TR an irresponsible imperialist.

The president took a broad view of his powers during the actual construction of the canal. If, as he once explained to his secretary of war, he should deem it best to place the three locks on the Pacific side at Miraflores instead of Sosa and dispense with the lake at Sosa by means of a broad sea-level channel, he would not hesitate to do so. But perhaps, he added with a caution always more visible in his acts than in his words, there should be added to the order the phrase "as recommended by the President and the Secretary of War," to avoid giving some congressman who wished to hamper the construction the chance to yell about not having followed the instructions of the legislators.

Although no president had up until then left the continental limits of the United States while in office, TR could not resist his desire to see the great project actually under construction, and he and his wife sailed for Panama on the USS *Louisiana* escorted by two other battleships. It was heady business, and he wrote: "It is a beautiful sight, these three great war vessels steaming southward in close column, and almost as beautiful at night when we see not only the lights but the loom through the darkness of the ships astern. . . . It seems a strange thing to think of my now being President, going to visit the work of the Panama Canal which I have made possible."

There was to be no nonsense, however, in Panamanian politics, however much that nation's independence had been recognized, that might interfere with the smooth working of the canal. In 1908, the last year of his second term, TR wrote sternly to Taft, then his secretary of war:

You are authorized to say to President Amador that the Government of the United States will consider any attempt at the election of a successor by fraudulent methods or methods which deny to a large part of the people opportunity to vote constitutes a disturbance of public order, which under Panama's constitution requires intervention, and this government will not permit the government of Panama to pass into the hands of anyone so elected.

Eight

John Morton Blum's careful study of TR's correspondence has made it clear how close a watch he kept on the appointments to state Republican committees and how deftly he constructed a personal organization within the party. As president he was always careful to consult the Republican senator of the state where any political appointment was to be made, but he also made sure it was understood that he was free to consult others as well. During his first term Senator Mark Hanna of Ohio, the old champion of McKinley, was still the dominant, or at least the rival, power in the party, and he had not only been opposed to Roosevelt but was known to be hankering for the next presidential nomination. TR's own fierce ambition for the same goal was accentuated by his distaste for owing his present elevation to an assassin's bullet; he yearned to be elected in his own right. After he had slowly but surely loosened Hanna's grip on the party, he was able to say, with a sigh of relief: "He has caused me a little worry but not much." Hanna's premature death suddenly eliminated this threat, and TR and his running mate, Senator Charles W. Fairbanks of Indiana, were easily nominated in the 1904 Republican convention and as easily elected the following fall. Running against a conservative Democratic candidate, Judge Alton B. Parker, Roosevelt polled 7.6 million votes, 56.4 percent of the popular vote to Parker's 37.6 percent, and swept the electoral college 336 to 140, carrying every state outside the South save the border state of Kentucky.

Industry and finance did not yet show the alarm about TR they were later to feel. Northern Securities had bothered them, but TR was still a Republican. Contributions to his campaign funds included $50,000 from Henry Clay Frick; $100,000 each from George J. Gould (son of Jay) and John Archbold (Standard Oil); and $150,000 from J. P. Morgan. The Republican treasurer, Cornelius Bliss, perhaps wisely, did not feel it necessary to inform the candidate of these.

TR, elated by his sweeping victory at the polls, felt at last that he had secured the confidence of the American people, and he became more open in the annunciation of his socially progressive principles, his "Square Deal," as it came to be known. In his annual message to Congress in 1905 he called for a pure food and drug law, supervision of insurance companies, investigation of child labor, an employers' liability law for the District of Columbia, and suits against railroad rebates.

He also made a public pronouncement that he was later bitterly to regret: "Under no circumstances will I be a candidate for or accept another nomination."

Race relations occupy so much of our news today that it is natural to inquire what TR did about them. There is no question that he found any sort of racial or religious discrimination odious, but there was far less that a president could do about them in his day than in ours. Indeed, there was very little he could do. The South was solid in its determination to maintain segregation; states' rights were deemed sacred, and the North was indifferent. TR could only express his helpless indignation at the counting of Negroes as part of the voting population without allowing them to vote: "It is an outrage that this one man [Congressman John S. Williams of Mississippi] should first be allowed to suppress the votes of three black men, and then to cast them himself in order to make his own vote the equal of that of four men." And he could only add, "To acquiesce in this state of things because it is not possible at the time to attempt to change it without doing damage is one thing. It is quite another to seem formally to approve it."

Early in his first term TR had invited Booker T. Washington to dine at the White House, which had aroused a howl of protest in newspapers throughout the South. Roosevelt's response was: "As things have turned out I am very glad that I asked him, for the clamor aroused by the act makes me feel as if the act was necessary. . . . I do not intend to offend the prejudices of anyone else, but neither do I allow their prejudices to make me false to my principles."

But in private he admitted that the invitation had been a political mistake, which he did not repeat, and today we might feel that he was going a bit far in not offending the prejudices of others. Witness, for example, this letter of his about the reappointment of three Negroes to political offices in Georgia:

The three best offices in Georgia are filled by colored men who have done their work admirably. High-grade whites feel outraged that these three best offices should be given to colored men, and if it were a case of original appointments I should, as a matter of wisdom, from the standpoint of both races, certainly not make more than one of the three a colored man. But to refuse to reappoint or continue in office a good servant simply because he is colored is an entirely different thing; yet it is wholly impossible to make this distinction clear to most thoroughly good men in Georgia.

The "thoroughly good" may stick in a modern throat, but that was the world TR had to face. We should give him credit for making it clear that his condemnation of discrimination was not limited to hostility against any one race:

There is nothing that I protest more strongly, socially and politically, than any proscription or looking down upon decent Americans because they are of Irish or German ancestry; but I protest just exactly as strongly against any similar discrimination against or sneering at men because they happen to be descended from people who came over here three centuries ago.

Where hate crimes, however, occurred in nations beyond his jurisdiction, he refused to indulge in idle protests or empty threats. Citing the Old West of his younger days where a man didn't draw a gun unless he was ready to shoot, he deplored the brandishing of weapons one had no idea of using. At a later time, during America's neutrality in the first years of World War I, he would accuse Wilson, in his relations with Germany, of shaking first his fist and then his finger. And now we find him writing Jacob Schiff about the persecution of Jews in Russia:

Why, my dear Mr. Schiff, the case was much simpler as regards the Armenians a few years ago. There the Turkish government was responsible and was able to enforce whatever was desired. The outrages on the Armenians were exactly the same as those perpetrated on the Jews of Russia, both in character and in extent. But we did not go to war with Turkey. Inasmuch as it was certain that our people would not go into such a war . . . it would have been worse than foolish to have threatened it, and not the slightest good would have been or was gained by any agitation which it was known would not be backed up by arms.

Nine

Since the beginning of 1904 Russia and Japan had been engaged in a savage war for supremacy in Northeast Asia. To the astonishment and awakening of the world Japan had emerged as a first-class military and naval power, sinking or capturing the bulk of the Russian fleet, taking Port Arthur, and driving deep into Manchuria. TR had at first favored Japan — Russia had antagonized America and much of Europe by her aggressiveness and arrogance in the Far East — but he now cast a wary eye on Tokyo as a potential opponent of American interests in the Pacific. It would be as well for everyone if Japan did not gain too sweeping a victory, and he decided to use such international influence as he had to procure a settlement.

The Japanese were certainly winning the war, but it was costing them dearly. Russia could always fall back on a seemingly infinite source of manpower if it chose and, as it appeared stubbornly willing to, drag on the conflict. Both sides, therefore, should have been open to overtures, and Roosevelt decided to approach the czar directly through his ambassador in St. Petersburg rather than deal with the prickly and proud Russian legate in Washington. After much jockeying for position both belligerents agreed to a peace conference in the United States, and TR was able to persuade them to pick Portsmouth, New Hampshire, over Washington, as the summer heat in the capital would hardly have been conducive to coolness of temper.

At this time John Hay, whom TR had inherited as secretary of state from McKinley, died and was replaced by Elihu Root, who had been TR's secretary of war before retiring to resume his highly successful law practice in New York. Hay had been a close friend of Roosevelt's as well as of his father, but the president had found him lacking in vigor and drive and was glad to have the services in state of Root, a brilliant and caustic attorney who, as Edith Roosevelt put it, was well qualified to give her husband advice because their characters were so different. Root knew how to keep TR's expansive imagination within reasonable bounds; he used his biting, sardonic humor with good effect on a chief who took it surprisingly well. But that is something always to keep in mind in any evaluation of Roosevelt: his reason was constantly at work, however unperceived, to balance the wildness of his words. At least until the last few years of his life.

The most difficult issue in the negotiations at Portsmouth was Japan's demand for an indemnity. Japan's emissaries finally agreed to drop the term *indemnity* as humiliating to Russia and instead call the sum demanded the price for half of Sakhalin Island, which Russia was to cede to Japan. The Russians, however, continued stubbornly to resist the imposition of any payment, and TR had to use all his powers of persuasion to convince the Japanese to be content with what they already had: control of Korea and Manchuria and a fleet doubled at the expense of the Russian navy. He also used the clinching argument that a continuation of the war would cost even a victor far more than any indemnity that could be extracted from a defeated enemy. What good would Siberia do for Japan even if she conquered it all?

Japan finally gave in, dropping all claim for an indemnity, and a treaty was concluded. Roosevelt in 1906 was deservedly awarded the Nobel Peace Prize. He accepted it gladly, but gave the money, forty thousand dollars, to a committee for industrial peace, writing to one of his sons:

I hate to do anything foolish or quixotic, and above all I hate to do anything that means the refusal of money which would ultimately come to you children. But Mother and I talked it over and came to the conclusion that while I was President, at any rate, and perhaps anyhow, I could not accept money given to me for making peace between two nations, especially since I was able to make peace simply because I was President.

TR's troubles with Japan were not concluded by the treaty. Even while it was being negotiated he had to face Japanese anger at the treatment of their emigrants in California. He never had patience with discrimination of any kind, but he found himself severely handicapped, as he did in the southern states that virtually disenfranchised the Negro by the limits of federal power in what were then deemed essentially state matters. One thing he could do, in view of the rise of the Japanese menace in the Pacific, was build up the navy, and this he did, making large annual demands of Congress. In 1908, for example, he requested authority to build four battleships, knowing the number would be halved, which it was, but also knowing it was the only way to get the needed two. In all he increased the navy from fifth in the world in size to second only to Britain's, with a total of twenty battleships, and in his second term he sent "the great white fleet" around the world to impress the powers that the United States was in a position to back up its word.

It was natural for him at times to express his exasperation at how much violent push was needed to persuade Americans to protect themselves, as when he wrote: "Most certainly the Japs are a wonderful people. I feel rather bitterly when I compare what they have done with the howling and whooping and yelling of our own people against even a moderate increase in our navy." And in 1908 he wrote: "I do not believe that there will be war with Japan, but I do believe there is enough chance of war to make it eminently wise to secure against it by building such a navy as to forbid Japan's hope for success. I happen to know that the Japanese military party is inclined for war with us and is not only confident of success, but confident that they could land a large expeditionary force in California and conquer all of the United States west of the Rockies. I fully believe that in the end they would pay dearly for this."

He was not only concerned with the

present status of the navy but was keenly concerned with its future. He went down on an early dive of the USS *Plunger*, one of our first submarines: "I went down in it chiefly because I didn't like to have the officers and enlisted men think I wanted them to try things I was reluctant to try myself. I believe a good deal can be done with these submarines, although there is always the danger of people getting carried away with the idea and thinking that they can be more use than they possibly could be."

Trouble in the Caribbean offered TR several opportunities to develop a new and wider concept of the Monroe Doctrine. When a Latin American nation defaulted in its financial obligations to one of the greater European powers, it had become an accepted remedy for the creditor country to send warships to intimidate and sometimes actually bombard the debtor nation. This was the case with Venezuela and Germany in 1902, but Roosevelt made it clear to the German ambassador that he would order Admiral Dewey to make sure that Germany did not take possession of any Venezuelan territory. When the ambassador gravely asked if the president realized the possible consequences of such an order, TR later claimed: "I answered that I had thoroughly counted the cost before I decided on the step, and asked him to look at the map, as a glance would show him that there was no place in the world where Germany in the event of conflict with the United States would be at a greater disadvantage than in the Caribbean Sea." Germany refrained from action, though some historians have thought that Roosevelt's account of it showed him as considerably more defiant than he had been.

At any rate, Europe and Latin America learned that the new Monroe Doctrine would not tolerate any European attempt to collect debts in our hemisphere by force. But a corollary to this was that the United States had an implied obligation to Europe to see that our small neighboring debtor states did not behave irresponsibly. When the government of Santo Domingo fell apart, Roosevelt assumed virtual control of the republic, appointing an American receiver and collector of customs, building roads, establishing schools, and creating a revenue service. It may have been for the good of Santo Domingo but it created howls of anti-imperialist resentment at home and throughout South America.

No charge is more often flung at Roosevelt than imperialism. Yet he never advocated an empire for the United States such as Britain, France, Portugal, Holland, and Germany conceived for themselves. It is true that we catch him in a letter written in 1895 to an old Civil War veteran saying: "If I were asked what the greatest boon I could confer on this nation was, I should answer, an immediate war with Great Britain for the conquest of Canada." But that was when he was allowing his always vivid imagination to visualize a single vast united nation covering everything on our continent north of the Mexican border. It was a concept that has intrigued many Americans; Canada wouldn't have been an empire but a group of additional states. TR never wished to keep Cuba or the Philippines; in each case he favored occupation to last only until the islands were ready for independence. The naval bases that he wanted — Hawaii, Guam, Cuba, Panama, and Puerto Rico — were not the bastions of empire but the necessary fueling spots for the warships that guaranteed the security of his country as preached by his mentor, Admiral Mahan.

Another example of TR's success in rather high-handed diplomacy is found in his management of the Alaskan-Canadian border dispute of 1903. Before the United States acquired Alaska, Britain and Russia had defined the line between British Columbia and the Alaskan Panhandle as running thirty miles inland from the head of tidewater. After the discovery of gold in the Klondike, Canada tried to alter this line to include the goldfields in its territory, but TR took a very firm position, generally now considered to have been justified by the facts, that he would not accept this and was willing to maintain the old border by force, if necessary. A compromise was sought of referring the matter to six arbitrators — three Americans, two Canadians, and one British. TR, being determined not to lose the decision by any such arrangement, appointed three arbitrators he could trust to vote as he wished, so that the result, if not favorable to the United States, would at least be a tie. The Americans voted as expected, as did the Canadians, but the British arbitrator, Lord Alverston, probably to avoid an international incident, took the American view, and the issue was peacefully settled.

Ten

France had bought off British and Italian interests in Morocco by promising them a free hand in Tripoli and Egypt, and the French Convention with Britain of April 1904 contemplated the ultimate division of Morocco between France and Spain. Germany and German interests were totally ignored, and the Kaiser's indignant retaliatory visit to Tangier provoked a war-threatening crisis. The Kaiser then proposed an international conference to settle the disputes and invited the American president to second his proposition to the nations concerned. TR, although dubious of the extent of America's involvement in the Mediterranean, agreed to do this on behalf of world peace, and the conference of thirteen nations duly assembled in the Andalusian port of Algeciras in Spain in 1906, with Henry White as the United States representative.

TR instructed White, whom he regarded as the ablest of American diplomats, "to keep friendly with all" but to do nothing to shake the recently concluded Franco-British entente, which he considered a force for peace in the troubled European scene. Basically TR was much more on the French than the German side. The prickliest issue facing the conference was the question of who should police Morocco, such policing being essential to the maintaining of the open-door agreement. The French, who had already been policing the territory for years and who had by far the greatest investment in Morocco, insisted on continuing their virtual control, willing only to share a bit of it with Spain, while the Germans wanted the policing confided to a group of smaller, neutral nations. Tempers flared, and the home capitals began to be heard from. The president of the Reichstag in Berlin made threatening speeches; the Paris press boiled. War loomed. White, believing that the Kaiser was not fully informed by his representative in the conference, now urged TR to go over the heads of the conference in a direct appeal to him.

TR agreed to do this, after inducing the French to make a final offer of minimum terms. They revised their position slightly by bringing the Sultan of Morocco into more direct relation with the French and Spanish police officers and associating Italy (a sop to Germany) in the police control. Germany continued to stand pat until TR, citing the Kaiser's letter to him of the previous June in which the German emperor had flatly stated: "I will in every case be willing to back up the decision which you consider to be the most fair and most practicable," insisting that the time had come for this promise to be fulfilled. The Kaiser gave in.

The Algeciras conference averted a war that would have come at a time when the French army was far less prepared for it than it would be in 1914. As Allan Nevins put it: "It allowed the powers a few more years in which to avert the great conflagration — years and opportunities which they threw away."

TR was entirely frank with Lodge about the individual and vital role he had played in the conference. "I became the intermediary between Germany and France," he wrote him. "This is a deep secret. . . . With Jusserand [French ambassador to the United States] I was able to go over the whole matter, and we finally worked out a conclusion which I think was entirely satisfactory. Do not let anyone except, of course, Nanny [Mrs. Lodge] know of this. Even Whitelaw Reid [ambassador to Britain] does not know it. I have told Taft but not Hay. I shall tell Root."

Eight years of peace was something, anyway, and the world owed them at least in part to TR. His relations with the Kaiser, contrary to what many thought, were always productive of concord. One can add the Venezuela crisis to Algeciras. Yet TR never made a secret of his admiration for virile nations, and the bristling, glittering, armored empire of William II was not unsympathetic to him until the brutal invasion of Belgium in 1914. He had even once gone so far as to express his understanding of Germany's ambition to become an imperial power. Writing how he would feel as a German about such a course of action, he stated: "I should adopt it without the least feeling that the Germans who advocated German colonial expansion were doing anything save what was right and proper from the standpoint of their own people. Nations may, and often must, have conflicting interests, and in the present age patriotism stands a good deal ahead of cosmopolitanism."

And in TR's rather condescending description of the politically liberal German-born Carl Schurz, he seems to betray a muffled respect for the Prussian aspects of Germany that Schurz repudiated:

He is not an American, and he is not a

present-day German. He is a leftover German of 1848, of the amiable, visionary, impractical, revolutionary type, now soured by his own constant wrong behavior for many years. He knows nothing whatever of modern Germany. . . . Modern Germany is alert, aggressive, military and industrial. It thinks it is a match for England and France combined in war, and would probably be less reluctant to fight both those powers together than they would be together to fight it.

TR was friendly and congenial with Baron H. S. von Sternberg and asked his legate in Berlin to urge his appointment as ambassador to the United States. There was considerable delay in this, perhaps in respect to former chancellor Bismarck's dictum: "I do not regard it as a virtue in my ambassadors to be popular in the nation to which they are accredited," but at last the appointment was made, and it facilitated relations between the two governments. In one of the last letters that TR wrote at the end of his second term he confided in the Kaiser: "It is very unlikely that I shall hold office again. But if — what I most earnestly hope may never occur — there should be a big war in which the United States was engaged, while I am still in bodily vigor, I should endeavor to get permission to raise a division of mounted rifles — cavalry in our use of the word, that is, nine regiments such as I commanded in the war with Spain."

Of course, there was such a war, but with his correspondent as the hated enemy, and he did indeed seek permission to raise such a regiment, only to be refused by President Wilson. There had always been a basic distrust behind TR's occasional admiration of the Kaiser. He had been flattered in 1910 by the latter's taking him on military maneuvers in Germany, a privilege not usually accorded to aliens, but from the beginning of their relationship he had deplored the Kaiser's rashness and excitability, so different from the cool reflectiveness behind his own seeming bluster. Henry Adams saw this, and when Lodge told him the British thought that Roosevelt was under the Kaiser's spell, he exclaimed: "For heaven's sake let them think so! The President's influence with the Kaiser is one of the strongest weapons we have in a really perilous condition. We know he understands the Kaiser, and that is enough."

Eleven

Roosevelt started his second term with resoundingly approving majorities in the nation and in Congress. There had also been enough scandals and public disclosures about the malefactions of wealth to engender considerable support for his "Square Deal." The age of muckraking had been initiated with the publication of Ida Tarbell's *History of the Standard Oil Company*. And furthermore the Standard Oil Company of Indiana had been exposed for cheating on rebates, as had the Sugar Trust for underpaying the U.S. customs by underweighing its imports at the docks.

Roosevelt wrote this to a friend about one of his campaign manager's unsuccessful efforts to raise money from E. H. Harriman:

> To this Harriman answered that . . . whenever it was necessary he could buy a sufficient number of senators and congressmen or state legislators to protect his interests, and when necessary he could buy the judiciary. These were his exact words. He did not say this under

any injunction of secrecy to Sherman and showed a perfectly cynical spirit of defiance throughout, his tone being that he greatly preferred to have in demagogues rather than honest men who treated them fairly, because when he needed he could purchase favors from the former.

In 1907 many were not surprised to hear the president in his annual message to Congress call for the imposition of income and inheritance taxes, the fixing of railroad rates based on the valuation of railroad property, currency reform, limitation of injunctions in labor disputes, extension of the eight-hour day, and control of campaign contributions.

Yet Roosevelt always kept a wary and suspicious eye on the radical left. "A government like ours," he wrote, "must equally dread the Scylla of mob rule and the reign of mere plutocracy," and even such a basic conservative as Elihu Root described him as "the great conservator of property and rights."

One of the signal accomplishments of the second term was the passage of the Hepburn Bill, which increased the regulating power of the Interstate Commerce Commission over railroads, giving it jurisdiction to inspect railroad records, to restrict rebates, and, to some degree, to establish rates charged. Senator Nelson W. Aldrich had tried to cripple these powers by giving the railroads ample opportunity to delay the commission's rulings indefinitely through appeals to the courts, but the bill provided for more summary legal action. It gave the federal courts the power to set aside any order of the commission, but provided for direct appeal to the Supreme Court and calendar priority in antitrust cases. TR eased off in his effort to obtain tariff reductions in order to reach a compromise in Congress on the Hepburn Bill.

In 1906 the Pure Food and Drug Act was passed to remedy the abuses of the meatpacking industry as exposed by Upton Sinclair's novel *The Jungle*. Finley Peter Dunne, "Mr. Dooley," described TR's reaction to the book: "Tiddy was toying with a light breakfast and idly turnin' over the pages iv the new book with both hands. Suddenly he rose fr'm the table, an cryin': 'I'm pizened,' began throwin' sausages out iv the window."

The Panic of 1907 was initiated by the failure of the Knickerbocker Trust Company in New York, which set off a run on banks and threatened a major financial disaster. The leading financiers of the day met in J. P. Morgan's library to discuss ways and means to avert the crash. The great banker sat in their midst, among his art treasures, silently playing solitaire while they suggested, one after another, possible steps to take, only to receive an abrupt negative shake of the head. At last a plan was evolved whereby a major brokerage house, Moore and Schley, whose imminent bankruptcy dangerously loomed, could be saved. It held substantial stock in the Tennessee Coal & Iron Company as collateral for loans, though the price had plummeted. If U.S. Steel exchanged some of its stock for the Tennessee stock, the solidly valuable steel shares would satisfy the Moore and Schley creditors, the brokerage house would be saved, and the financial crisis averted. And so in the end it turned out. But U.S. Steel insisted on an assurance from the federal government that the control of Tennessee, which the transaction would provide, would not subject it to an antitrust suit. TR was consulted and gave the requested assurance. Following the adage that no good deed goes unpunished, he would later find himself bitterly criticized for assisting U.S. Steel to increase its monopoly by this (as it turned out) highly advantageous acquisition of Tennessee.

TR had earlier, at the bringing of the Northern Securities suit, accused Morgan of presuming to deal on equal terms with the U.S. government. To many observers in 1907 it looked as if that was exactly what Morgan was successfully doing.

Roosevelt marred the end of his term with one foolish act. When Joseph Pulitzer's paper *The World* accused him of "deliberate misstatements of fact" in defending his Panamanian policy, he insisted that his attorney general institute a suit for criminal libel. Of course, the suit was lost, and TR had to content himself with one of his angriest denunciations: "Pulitzer is one of these creatures of the gutter of such unspeakable degradation that to him even eminence on a dunghill seems enviable."

McKinley had appointed William Howard Taft as governor of the Philippine Islands, a post that TR had wanted for himself at the time he had been offered the vice presidential nomination. TR kept a sharp eye on Taft, therefore, after TR became president, and ultimately promoted him to be secretary of war, where he was extremely helpful in the construction of the Panama Canal, carried out under the aegis of the army. Searching the political field for a successor, Roosevelt, who had barred a third term for himself, decided that his two likeliest candidates were Taft and Root.

Taft was fifty-one in 1908, the last full year of TR's second term. A native of Ohio, he had been in public life for twenty-one years, as a prosecuting attorney and then judge in his home state and thereafter in the federal offices above stated. Because of his obesity and genial personality he appeared to the public mind as a kind of Santa Claus figure, smiling, easygoing, tolerant, beaming the rays of his benevolent heart on people whom he could not imagine to be any less benevolent than himself. If there was a political gain in this — something comparable to the popularity that Ronald Reagan in our time achieved — there was also a political liability. Was such a man really capable of leading the nation in a grave crisis? Might he not be too weak or easily misled or careless of significant detail?

Taft in fact was a shrewd and conscientious worker, fully capable of command. He had been the effective governor of Pacific islands teeming with revolt and the efficient and respected head of our army. His real political liability lay in his deep distaste for the smoke-filled back rooms of practical politics and in his yearning for the intellectual isolation of the judicial bench. Roosevelt saw this, but tried to entice him toward the presidency by pointing out how effective a chief of state he might prove if he would only make his affability the partner of his willpower:

> Let the audience see you smile, *always,* because I feel that your nature shines out so transparently when you do smile — you big, generous, high-minded fellow. Moreover, let them realize the truth, which is that for all your gentleness and kindliness and generous good nature, there never existed a man who was a better fighter when the need arose.

It is a tribute to Taft's good nature that in later years, after the acerbic animosity aroused by the Bull Moose campaign, Roosevelt forgave him, as he never forgave the colder, more calculating but preeminently just Elihu Root. The three men had been close friends and allies in the years when one of them had been in the White House and two in his cabinet. They had even called themselves the three musketeers and sometimes signed themselves accordingly: D'Artagnan, of course, for Roosevelt, Athos for the sober and cynical Root, and Porthos for stout Taft. Yet all must have known that Aramis and not D'Artagnan was the third musketeer. Making D'Artagnan one may have prefigured the breakup.

Root, though he backed Taft, may have toyed with the idea of seeking the successorship to Roosevelt for himself, but he knew — and TR knew — that a man whose public image was that of a corporate lawyer for big business could never be elected. Taft, who might genuinely have preferred the choice to fall on Root, also had to acknowledge this, as he recalled a conversation with Roosevelt: "The President was particular to say to Root, so the President told me, that he was committed to me for the presidency so far as his influence might properly go, and I infer that Root had no definite intention of running for that office, though you never can tell."

But what Taft really wanted was something quite different:

> My ambition . . . is to become a justice of the Supreme Court. I presume, however, there are very few men who would refuse to accept the nomination of the Republican Party for the presidency, and I am not an exception. If it were to come

to me with the full understanding of the party of the weaknesses that I should have as a candidate, I should not feel that I had any right to decline, and should make the best fight possible to secure my election.

Roosevelt was fully aware of Taft's preference and was both fair and reasonable about it. He not only offered him the seat of retiring associate justice Henry Brown; he promised him that if he were still in office when the chief justiceship became vacant he would elevate him to that post. But he nonetheless still urged him to run for president as his primary duty to the nation:

As I see the situation it is this. There are strong arguments against your taking this justiceship. In the first place my belief is that of all the men that have appeared so far you are the man who is most likely to receive the Republican presidential nomination and who is, I think, the best man to receive it and under whom we would have the best chance to succeed. . . . The good you could do in four or eight years as the head of the nation would be incalculable.

Mrs. Helen Taft may have been the deciding influence. She was strongly and articulately in favor of her husband's running. When he at last consented and started campaigning for the nomination she urged him to soft-pedal his endorsement of TR's social program, which is certainly interesting in view of what later happened. She wrote her husband:

> I do hope that you are not going to make any more speeches on the Roosevelt policies, as I think the matter should be left alone for the present — and you are simply aiding and abetting the President in keeping things stirred up. Let the corporations rest for a while. It is soon enough to talk about it when something needs to be done, and, whatever the West may be, in the East it has an aggressive air.

It is hard not to suppose that Roosevelt saw in Taft a future president whom he could dominate or at least one who would always seek to avail himself of the wisdom gained by longer experience in the job. At any rate, he threw the entire crushing weight of his own prestige and popularity into the fight for Taft's nomination in 1908 and with it the voices of the party members whose loyalty he had gained in seven years of astute political handling.

Lodge, chairman of the Republican convention, paced the platform for twenty minutes while the delegates howled their enthusiasm for Roosevelt, crying "Four years more!" When the tumult at last died down, he quelled the surge toward his friend's nomination with a few cold and decisive words:

His refusal of a nomination, dictated by the loftiest motives and by a noble loyalty to American traditions, is final and irrevocable. Anyone who attempts to use his name as a candidate for the Presidency impugns both his sincerity and his good faith, two of the President's greatest and most conspicuous qualities, upon which no shadow has ever been cast.

Taft was now easily nominated and easily defeated William Jennings Bryan in the election that fall, polling 51.6 percent of the popular vote to Bryan's 43 percent and winning the electoral vote 321 to 162.

It was a pity that TR, whose record on race relations was a good one for his day, should have clouded it by his action in an incident in 1906. In the border town of Brownsville, Texas, some twenty armed men engaged in a shooting riot that resulted in the wounding of one man and the killing of another. The townspeople accused members of the all-black Twenty-sixth Infantry Regiment of having instigated the riot in revenge for some racial slurs. Defenders of the regiment accused the town of staging the riot to discredit the blacks. On interrogation the entire regiment refused to testify, and all three companies, a total of 167 men, were discharged from the army "without honor." The sentence, though vigorously criticized, was not overturned by the president, though ultimately fourteen of the men were allowed to reenlist. TR became very indignant when people questioned his judgment in the case, insisting that he would have acted in the same fashion had the regiment been all white, but that was not the way it was generally viewed, and it may be significant that he made no mention of the incident in his autobiography.

An interesting difference between Roosevelt's campaign in 1904 and Taft's four years later is in the treatment of contributions from business interests. In TR's time it was still considered improper and undignified for a sitting president to barnstorm the country. TR, of course, had found this attitude very trying; he likened it to "lying still under shell fire," as he had experienced during the war in Cuba. But it heightened the importance of political contributions, and in 1904, as we have seen, the "malefactors of great wealth" had not yet been scared out of their traditional support of the Republican Party and gave heavily to TR's campaign. These payments may have been concealed from Roosevelt, but in any event he proved much less sensitive on the subject in 1908 than the actual candidate.

Federal law at the time forbade political contributions from corporations but was silent about those from corporate officers or directors. When William Nelson Cromwell, the notorious lawyer who had helped to engineer the Panamanian revolt for a huge fee, offered Taft the sum of fifty thousand dollars, the candidate insisted that it be lowered to ten thousand dollars. This may seem a dubious kind of laundering, but at least it was a step in the right moral direction. TR thought it overscrupulous and wrote:

> You blessed old trump, I have always said you would be the greatest president, bar only Washington and Lincoln, and I

feel mighty inclined to strike out the exceptions. My affection and respect for you are increased by your attitude about contributions. But really I think you are oversensitive.

George R. Sheldon, the party treasurer, would have deemed this a masterpiece of understatement when he received Taft's direction to accept no contributions from representatives of Standard Oil or from any officer or director of a company that might in Taft's term of office face prosecution under the Sherman Antitrust Act or other federal law.

"I would like to have an ample fund to spread the light of Republicanism," Taft wrote TR, "but I am willing to undergo the disadvantage to make certain that in the future we shall reduce the power of money in politics for unworthy purposes."

When Sheldon demanded where, under such restrictions, he was expected to raise the funds needed to defeat the populist William Jennings Bryan, who was again the Democratic nominee, Taft told him to go after the smaller businesses. He did so and collected $1.6 million less than the $2.2 million raised in 1904, but enough to win the election. Perhaps the scarecrow of Bryan had frightened enough of the middle class to elect his opponent even without the aid of the moguls.

Taft's acceptance speech at the Republican convention may have epitomized his go-slow policy in implementing TR's Square Deal:

> The chief function of the administration, in my judgment, is distinct from, and a progressive element of that which has been performed by President Roosevelt. The chief function of the next administration is to complete and perfect the machinery . . . by which lawbreakers may be promptly restrained and punished, but which shall operate with sufficient accuracy and dispatch to interfere with legitimate business as little as possible.

And Taft's letter to TR after the farewell White House dinner to the outgoing president on March 3, 1909, expressed already what sounds like an only pious hope:

> People have attempted to represent that you and I were in some way at odds during the last three months, whereas you and I know that there has not been

the slightest difference between us, and I welcome the opportunity to stay the last night of your administration under the White House roof to make as emphatic as possible the refutation of any such suggestion.

Twelve

Gifford Pinchot was the handsome, patrician, ambitious, and idealistic son of a rich father who encouraged him to undertake the extensive training that would enable him to achieve his ambition of becoming America's first professional forester. Initially employed in 1892 to manage the forest on George W. Vanderbilt's immense estate in Asheville, North Carolina, he proved his metal by reducing expenses to a minimum through the expedient of selective logging: excluding cattle from the forest (he called them "horned locusts") and cutting only the trees that shaded the younger still-growing ones. He was soon called to government work in Washington, and in 1898 he was named chief of the Division of Forestry under the jurisdiction of the General Land Office in the Department of the Interior. The Land Office was totally incompetent to manage a cornfield, let alone a forest, but young Pinchot would soon enough change all that.

TR, as newly elected governor of New York, now called on Pinchot for a plan to manage the forests of that state, and he went to Albany. As Pinchot wrote in his memoirs: "I laid before the governor my plan for a single-headed New York Forest Commission instead of the spineless, many-headed commission of those days, and he approved it entirely. TR and I did a little wrestling at which he beat me; and some boxing during which I had the honor of knocking the future President of the United States off his very sturdy pins."

It was the beginning of a friendship, not only of vital importance to the history of American conservation but to the story of the breakup of TR's friendship with Taft and the split in the Republican Party.

Roosevelt called for Pinchot's assistance almost immediately after taking office as president. It is believed that Pinchot contributed this portion of TR's first State of the Union address:

The fundamental idea of forestry is the perpetuation of forests by use. Forest protection is not an end in itself; it is a means to increase and sustain the resources of our country and the industries which depend upon them. The preservation of our forests is an imperative business necessity. We have come to see clearly that whatever destroys the forest, except to make way for agriculture, threatens our well-being.

Pinchot, throughout Roosevelt's two terms, was a power in the land. He never obtained cabinet rank, but he had constant access to the president, who always listened to him, and that, as in the case of Harry Hopkins under FDR or Colonel House under Wilson, was all he needed to implement his projects.

They were sorely needed. Of 250 billion board feet of national timber, 40 billion were being cut annually and replaced by only 10 billion. The president could map out areas of the public domain and declare them natural forestland and subject their new occupants, homesteaders or lumber interests, to regulations of yield cutting, cattle grazing, irrigation, and other protective restrictions.

Pinchot's interests as a naturalist were much narrower than Roosevelt's. He did not share the latter's passionate and expertly informed enthusiasm for birds or beasts. When Roosevelt claimed to have been the last person to spot a passenger pigeon in the wild, the ornithologists believed him. Nor did Pinchot share, at least to anything like the same degree, TR's reveling in beautiful nature. He was not as bad as "Uncle Joe" Cannon, representative from Illinois and long-term Speaker of the House, who wouldn't vote a cent for "scenery," but his philosophy was distinctly utilitarian. He wanted to make the forests useful to man. And he reached out beyond government to the owners of vast private forests to join as many of them as he could in the Society of American Foresters to spread knowledge of how to prevent and contain forest fires and how to provide power sites for water and electricity.

Pinchot and TR addressed the problem of water shortage in the arid lands of the West. Aided by Senator Francis Newlands of Nevada they worked for the passage of the Reclamation Act of 1902 whereby the proceeds of the sale of certain lands in the public domain would be allotted by the secretary of the interior for irrigation projects.

When Roosevelt took office there was no protection for wildlife except in national parks. In 1903 he declared Pelican's Island in Florida, once a teeming source of bird mating but subsequently abandoned because of hunters, the first national wildlife refuge, and three years later he created six more. Edith Roosevelt joined her husband in the denunciation of women who wore egrets' plumes in their hats. "If anything," her husband wrote to a bird lover, "Mrs. Roosevelt feels more strongly than I do."

In 1905 Pinchot achieved his goal of transferring the Division of Forestry, of which, of course, he was chief, from the Department of the Interior to the more sympathetic and knowledgeable one of Agriculture. But his difficulties with the former, as we shall tragically see, were not over.

Although TR, as we have seen, was no great enthusiast for the American Indian — at least while they were still in belligerent opposition to westward-moving white men — he had a great respect for their reservations and origins once they had been quelled. He even obtained the passage of the National Monuments Act to preserve their tribal relics.

Toward the end of TR's second term the opposition to his conservation policies, which had long rumbled, became fierce. Homesteaders who claimed that too much land in the pubic domain was set aside for grazing, and lumber interests that maintained too much was set aside for forests, were now listened to by congressmen, and there was even some wild talk in parts of the far West of secession. The government went down to defeat in its fight for the establishment of an Inland Waterways Commission to regulate navigation, irrigate arid lands, protect low areas from flooding, and supply water for domestic and manufacturing purposes.

Worse was to come. A bill was introduced in Congress to deprive the president of his power to create national forests from the public domain in the states of Colorado, Idaho, Montana, Oregon, Washington, and Wyoming. Knowing it was sure to pass and with only a few days to lose, TR sent Pinchot to map out areas that he could nominate as forestland while he still had the power to do so. Pinchot laid out thirty-three such areas, and the president thus added sixteen million acres to forestland — to the fury of the lumber interests.

Despite all opposition, Roosevelt as president increased our national forests from 42 million acres to 172 million and created fifty-one national wildlife refuges. As Senator Robert La Follette said of him: "His greatest work was actually beginning a world movement to staying terrestrial waste."

Thirteen

This chapter will be devoted to quotations from TR's correspondence during his two terms as president. I hope to illustrate the diversity of his interests even while he was concentrating his principal energies on a job that affected not only the nation but the planet itself.

We start with his private injunction to a naval officer who, although promoted, had a drinking problem:

> But for your own sake and for the sake of the service which is so dear to us both I wish greatly that you would write me pledging your word as an officer and a gentleman that you would never again under any circumstances permit yourself to get under the influence of liquor.

When he discovered that the tax on the New York City residence of his cabinet officer Elihu Root had been suddenly and steeply raised, he responded with his usual anger and suspicion, writing Mayor Seth Low as follows:

What the tax commissioners mean or can mean I do not know, but it seems literally impossible that they could have proceeded from any other than a sinister motive in this attack upon, and outrageous discrimination against, a singularly upright, self-sacrificing and disinterested public servant.

TR, although born and bred in the heart of what was then considered the best and most exclusive New York society, had little use for its showy and party-loving side, as exemplified by Newport and Mrs. Astor and the list of four hundred eligible family names compiled by her majordomo, Ward McAllister. That TR's daughter, Alice, who loved him but loved to defy him, cultivated this world no doubt caused this snort of disgust:

Personally the life of the Four Hundred in its typical form strikes me as being as flat as stale champagne. I would rather hold my own in any congenial political society — even in Tammany — than in a circle where Harry Lehr is deemed a prominent and rather fascinating person.

It could have been only through Alice that

TR would so much as have heard the name of Harry Lehr, the epicene court jester of first Mrs. Astor and then Mrs. Stuyvesant Fish. And it may have been the raised — and dropped — question of Alice's presentation at the Court of St. James that elicited this comment:

I have grown to have a constantly increasing horror of the Americans who go abroad desiring to be presented at court or to meet sovereigns. In very young persons it is excusable folly; in older people it is mere snobbishness.

And here is his sharp summary judgment of the kind of socialite who tended, if he was willing to work at all, to go into the diplomatic service. He is referring to Lawrence Townsend, his minister to Belgium.

He possesses all the superficial requirements of the minister, and none that are of the slightest consequence when there is any real work to be done. He is a gentleman. He speaks foreign languages. He knows the minutiae of diplomacy, and he has a beautiful wife who, as a matter of fact, got him his present position and expects to keep him in it. All kinds of social and some political pressure is exercised on his behalf. But he is in the office not because he can do good to the service but because the office does good to him, and he has no claim whatever on retention — which is equally true of four-fifths of our European ambassadors and ministers.

TR had made his good friend Bellamy Storer ambassador to Austria, and the latter's ultimate recall had not been because of his incapacity in the job but his incapacity to control his wife, an ardent Catholic who used her position to promote appointments in ecclesiastical politics. She was born a Longworth and was the aunt of TR's son-in-law, Nicholas. Here is TR's last stern warning, addressed directly to her:

If you cannot make up your mind absolutely to alter your conduct in this regard, while your husband is in the diplomatic service, to refrain absolutely from taking any further part in the matter of ecclesiastical politics at the Vatican and to refuse to write or speak to anyone (whether laymen or ecclesiastics — at home or abroad) as you have been writing and speaking in the Cardinal's hat matter, then Bellamy cannot with propriety continue to remain Ambassador of the United States.

Another example of a reprimand, although far less severe, is this one to the writer Upton Sinclair. His novel *The Jungle*, about the horrible conditions in the Chicago meatpacking industry, had aroused both the nation and its president, but his violent language even for a good cause sometimes overstated the truth.

I must add that you do not seem to feel bound to avoid making and repeating utterly reckless statements which you have failed to back up by proof. But my own duty is entirely different. I am bound to see that nothing but the truth appears, that this truth does in its entirety appear, and that it appears in such shape that practical results for good will follow.

His interest in wildlife did not flag, and he was never too busy to concern himself with the welfare of the bears in Yellowstone:

There are lots of tin cans in the garbage heaps which the bears muss over, and it has now become fairly common for a bear to get his paw so caught in a tin can that he cannot get if off, and of course great pain and injury follow.

Less concern about pain caused to animals is shown in this description of a wolf hunt on a presidential vacation in Colorado in 1905:

> I was in at the death of eleven wolves. . . . I never took part in a row which ended in the death of a wolf without getting through the run in time to see the death. . . . One run was nine miles long, and I was the only man in at the finish except the professional wolf hunter Abernathy, who is really a wonderful fellow, catching the wolves alive by thrusting his gloved hands down between their jaws so they cannot bite.

Nor was he averse to contemplating the relationship of such carnivores to men, and to himself:

> Yet wide and deep though the gulf is between even the lowest man and an anthropoid ape, or some carnivore as intelligent as a dog, there are in both the latter animals and in a good many higher

animals intellectual traits and (if I may use the word loosely) moral traits which represent embryonic or rudimentary forms of such intellectual and moral traits of our own and perhaps prefigure them.

The fierceness of man was in TR's opinion the raw material out of which a soldier had to be carved, and he charged the prating of antiwar idealists with producing "a habit of mind under the effect of which the military or warlike virtues tend to atrophy." When he organized his Rough Riders he called on all the virtues of the frontier:

> I was immensely struck by the superiority of the man who had been bred in the open, or was accustomed to the open, who knew how to take cover and to handle horse and rifle, over the ordinary clerk or mechanic or similar individual from the great industrial centers.

Despite his Southern blood and his pride in the naval accomplishments of his maternal uncles, TR remained adamant in his strong condemnation of the folly and belligerence of the Southerners who in his opinion had plunged the nation into civil strife. He wrote to a friend who maintained that there were two sides to every quarrel:

Perhaps I should bar one sentence — that in which you say that in no quarrel is the right all on one side and the wrong all on the other. As regards the actual act of secession, the actual opening of the Civil War, I think the right was exclusively with the Union people and the wrong exclusively with the secessionists; and indeed I do not know of another struggle in history in which the sharp division between right and wrong can be made in quite so clear-cut a manner.

This opinion he held in spite of his disapproval of Northern abolitionists and their violent agitation against slavery:

In social and economic, as in political reforms, the violent revolutionary extremist is the worst friend of liberty, just as the arrogant and intense reactionary is the worst friend of order. It was Lincoln, and not Wendell Phillips and the fanatical abolitionists, who was the effective champion of union and freedom.

In his reading of the Victorian novelists TR was always guarded in his appreciation of Dickens:

There are innumerable characters that he has created which symbolize vices, virtues, follies and the like, almost as well as the characters in Bunyan; and therefore I think the wise thing to do is simply to skip the bosh and twaddle and vulgarity and untruth and get the benefit out of the rest. Of course, one fundamental difference between Thackeray and Dickens is that Thackeray was a gentleman and Dickens was not.

And he always found time for Greek tragedy:

I have never been able to see that there was the slightest warrant for resenting the death of Agamemnon on the part of his son and daughter, inasmuch as the worthy gentleman had previously slain another daughter, to whose loss the brother and sister never even allude; not to mention that he had obtained possession of the daughter, in order to slay her, by treachery, and that he had brought Cassandra home with him as his mistress.

We catch a glimpse of TR's ability to synchronize his knowledge of history with the names and official positions of his guests at a White House entertainment:

At the state dinner Prince Louis of Battenberg [a British admiral] sat between me and Bonaparte [Charles Joseph, TR's secretary of the navy], and I could not help smiling to myself that here was this British admiral seated beside this American Secretary of the Navy, being a grandnephew of Napoleon and the grandson of Jerome, King of Westphalia; while the British admiral was the grandson of a Hessian general who was the subject of King Jerome and served under Napoleon, and then, by no means creditably, deserted him in the middle of the Battle of Leipzig.

It is perhaps time for a more domestic note. Young Quentin and three of his pals on a frolicsome afternoon put spitballs on some of the White House portraits.

I did not discover it until after dinner, and then pulled Quentin out of bed and had him take them all off the portraits, and this morning required him to bring in the three other culprits before me. I explained to them that they had acted like boors, that it would have been a disgrace to have behaved so in any gentleman's house, but that it was a double disgrace in the house of the Nation. . . . They were four very sheepish small boys when I got through with them!

I would like to end these quotations to show how charming TR could be when the occasion called for it. The acting American governor of Cuba, prior to its independence, had sent Mrs. Roosevelt the Christmas present of a pitcher and basin. Perhaps because of the impropriety of such a gift from a governor to his chief, it had to be returned, but Edith had liked it, and her husband wished to keep it for her. He wrote the governor:

But the fact is, my dear Governor, that the pitcher and basin are so very beautiful that I simply cannot bear not to give them to her myself, and, after all, altho I shall have to make you permit me to pay for them . . . the major part of the gift, that is, the trouble in finding it, and the taste in choosing it, cannot but be yours, and so you have simply put us *both* under an obligation.

Fourteen

The retired president, accompanied by his son Kermit, headed for Africa to make a ten months' safari that had long been one of his dreams. The most dangerous animal he had so far hunted was the grizzly bear, and he yearned to try his luck and skill with the lion, the elephant, the rhino, and the cape buffalo. Conscious of his reputation as one who put a bullet through the heart of every wild thing he encountered, and anxious to ameliorate it with one as a conservationist, he dedicated his safari to the cause of science and emphasized to the press that the animals shot would be stuffed and added to the collection of the Natural History Museum in Washington. He persuaded Andrew Carnegie to finance the expedition, which the latter did on a munificent scale with a staff of 260 bearers, cooks, and tent men to accompany Roosevelt and the scientists he had invited to join him. TR also, on his own behalf, contracted for fifty thousand dollars with a magazine to send articles about the trip as it progressed.

He was more tickled than his wife, who of course would be left behind, by some of the newspaper accounts of the forthcoming trip: "I was immensely amused the other day to see an article in the *Philadelphia Ledger* in which the writer stated that as I had had a very picturesque career, and as it was probably now at an end, it would really be a fitting, and on the whole, a happy conclusion if I came to my death in some striking way on the African trip!"

And J. P. Morgan is supposed to have raised his glass at dinner to the toast: "America expects that every lion will do his duty."

The expedition traversed Kenya and ended in Khartoum. It was estimated that TR and his son shot some three hundred animals, and that TR was personally responsible for nine lions, eight elephants, twenty zebras, seven giraffes, and six buffaloes. Some of the accounts he sent home were sufficiently thrilling:

> Right in front of me, thirty yards off, there appeared from behind the bushes which had first screened him from my eyes, the tawny galloping form of a big maneless lion. Crack! — the Winchester spoke; and as the soft-nosed bullet ploughed forward through his flank the lion swerved so that I missed him with

the second shot; but my third bullet went through the spine and forward into his chest. Down he came sixty yards off, his hind quarters dragging, his head up, his ears back, but his jaws open and lips drawn up in a prodigious snarl, as he endeavored to turn and face us.

Edith met the travelers in Khartoum, and she and her husband now embarked on a six-week tour of European capitals where they were greeted by enthusiastic crowds and royalty. There was a slight hitch in Rome where Pius X made the granting of an interview conditional on the Roosevelts' not visiting the American Methodist Mission, which TR refused, but King Victor Emmanuel of Italy received him, and another near hitch in Berlin when TR declined to stay in the royal palace unless Edith too was invited. The Kaiser, however, relaxed his rule; both Roosevelts were included, and TR was asked to join his host at a mock army battle staged for the American ex-president's amusement and perhaps edification.

The Roosevelts' stay in London was marred by the death of Edward VII, and TR was asked to represent President Taft at the obsequies. He was also able to comfort and reassure Queen Alexandra, who had appealed to him in her intense grief to delay what seemed to her the too hasty inhumation of her husband's corpse.

He wrote Lodge:

I drive through dense throngs of people cheering and calling, exactly as if I were President and visiting cities at home where there was great enthusiasm for me. As I say, I have been much puzzled by it. It is largely because, and perhaps exclusively because, I am a former President of the American Republic which stands to the average European as a queer attractive dream, being sometimes regarded as a golden Utopia partially realized, and sometimes as a field for wild adventure of a by no means necessarily moral type — in fact a kind of mixture of Bacon's Utopia and Raleigh's Spanish Main.

Roosevelt's return to America onboard the *Kaiserin Augusta Victoria* was another triumph. The banks and docks of New York Harbor were lined with shouting crowds to welcome the great vessel from whose bridge the beaming ex-president cheerfully waved. Six battleships and hundreds of small craft

148

were assembled to greet him, and a twenty-one-gun salute boomed from Fort Wadsworth.

Yet he was not quite the same man who had departed the country a year before. Archie Butt, the devoted naval aide who was later to lose his life on the *Titanic,* noticed this.

> He was just the same in manner, in appearance, in expression, yet there was something different. We, all of us who had been closely associated with him in the past, felt it. . . . To me he had ceased to be an American, but had become a world citizen. His horizon seemed to be greater, his mental scope more encompassing. . . . He is bigger, broader, capable of greater good or greater evil, I don't know which, than when he left.

Nicholas Murray Butler, the president of Columbia University, had struck a note of truth years before, when he had warned TR that he would find it harder to be an ex-president than a president.

Fifteen

It was inevitable that the new president should expect to be better served by his own appointees than by his predecessor's, and understandable that he should not feel he had to consult with his predecessor as to their selection, yet Roosevelt was indignant at what he considered the arbitrary replacement of worthy men. Nor did he at all approve of the fact that six out of nine of Taft's cabinet secretaries were lawyers who had represented large corporations and might be expected to prefer a financial climate agreeable to their former clients. Taft's abrupt removal of Henry White as ambassador to France because (and this was believed by both Lodge and Root) he had failed, decades previously, when White was first secretary at the London embassy, to procure tickets to a House of Commons debate for the honeymooning Tafts, must have disgusted TR who regarded White not only as a close friend but as America's ablest diplomat.

Both Taft and his wife were capable of occasional smallnesses, but it seems more likely that Helen Taft was the one who bore a grudge against White. She certainly bore one against Roosevelt, and what could be more natural? There had always been more than a hint of condescension in TR's attitude toward his chosen successor, whom he once described as "a kindly and well-meaning man with no instinct for leadership," a note of "Now I've done the bulk of the job and shown you the way, carry on!" She wanted her husband, of whom she was naturally proud and possessive, to stand on his own feet and have his own niche in history, and she found the long shadow of his predecessor oppressive.

But the real personal blow to Roosevelt was in Taft's discharge of Pinchot, the ex-president's particular protégé and friend, as chief of the Division of Forestry. This came about after Pinchot had challenged the sale by Richard Ballinger, secretary of the interior, of certain lands in the public domain to a Guggenheim family syndicate. Taft had upheld the action of his cabinet officer, and Pinchot had thereupon written an open letter to Senator J. A. Dolliver of Iowa defending his position. Elihu Root, now a senator from New York, sat with a committee that upheld the president, and he advised Taft, who had served with him in TR's cabinet and was a close Republican ally, that "there is only one thing for you to do now, and you must do it at once," which was to discharge Pinchot for insubordination. And Taft did so.

It was, of course, inevitable that liberals and TR himself should see this as the revenge of lumber interests against the man who had deprived them of so much of their prey. Root himself admitted that the affair was "pregnant of immense evil," both to the administration and to the Republican Party. Had he known how much, even as strict a man as himself might have been inclined to overlook even so glaring an example of political insubordination.

Roosevelt was waxing cooler and cooler about his successor. He made supporting speeches for Republican candidates for Congress in the 1910 midterm elections, but he voiced his deepening doubts in a letter to Root:

> The sordid business of most of the so-called Regulars, who now regard themselves as especially the Taft men, and the wild, irresponsible folly of the ultra-Insurgents, make a situation which is very unpleasant. From a variety of causes, the men who are both sane and progressive, the men who make up the

strength of the party, have been left so at sea during these months in which Taft has put himself in commission of Aldrich, Cannon, Ballinger and Wickersham, that they have themselves tended to become either sordid on the one hand or wild on the other. I do not see how as a decent citizen I could have avoided taking the stand I have taken this year, and striving to unite the party and to help the Republicans to retain the control of Congress and of the State of New York, while at the same time endeavoring to see that this control within the party was in the hands of sensible and honorable men who were progressives and not of a Bourbon reactionary type.

Root was in the difficult position of trying to keep peace between Taft and Roosevelt and save the party from a split. TR still had faith and trust in Root. In a letter to Andrew Carnegie about world peace he said of Root:

You know how I trust him; he was the man of my cabinet, the man on whom I relied, to whom I owed most, the greatest Secretary of State we have ever had, as great a cabinet officer as we ever had, save Alexander Hamilton alone. He is as sane and cool-headed as he is high-minded; he neither lets facts blind him to ideals, nor ideals to facts; he is the wisest and safest of advisers and staunchly loyal alike to friends and causes — and all I say I mean, and it is said with the full remembrance that on certain points he and I would hardly agree.

I quote this in full for its contrast to TR's attitude three years later when he turned on his old friend.

There was certainly no question, at any rate, that TR had come to view Taft as the betrayer of all his progressive ideals, his so-called Square Deal, and this despite the fact that the Taft administration had achieved an eight-hour day for government employees, expanded the civil service, supported a constitutional amendment in favor of the income tax, and brought more antitrust suits, under Attorney General George W. Wickersham, including the one that broke up the Standard Oil Company, than in all of TR's two terms. Yet a considerable part of the public agreed with the former president. Taft was widely seen as less zealous than his predecessor in his opposition to business monopoly, and his support of the protective tariff in the interest of Wall Street strongly intensified this feeling. The Payne-Aldrich Tariff Bill, sponsored by Congressman Sereno W. Payne and Rhode Island senator Nelson W. Aldrich, staunch supporters of big business, was publicly endorsed by the president as "the best tariff law the Republicans ever made and therefore the best the country ever had." What this statement cost Taft in public esteem was gained in his higher reputation with the right-wing Republican Party machine and with Joseph G. Cannon, "Uncle Joe," Speaker of the House, who had served in Congress for half a century.

The progressives in the Republican Party, now frankly labeling themselves that, began to rally around Roosevelt, hoping to nominate him instead of Taft at the 1912 convention in Chicago. But, as TR still hesitated to declare himself, they turned to Senator Robert M. La Follette of Wisconsin, an accredited liberal, whose "Wisconsin Idea" of reform encompassed control of party bosses and expansion of business regulating agencies. But La Follette suffered a brief but politically fatal mental collapse in February of that year, and the governors of seven states appealed to the still wavering Roosevelt.

His wavering was not caused by any false

modesty. He was troubled, of course, by his 1905 declaration that he would never accept another nomination, but this should have been discounted as meaning his decision not to run for a third *consecutive* term, on the plausible theory that a president still in office at the end of his second term had, in a now solidly established government bureaucracy, an unfair advantage over any opponent. But TR's real trouble lay in going against the man whom he had all but named as his successor, dividing the party and, perhaps greatest of all, flying in the face of the heartfelt advice of his closest personal and political friends, Root and Lodge.

In favor of running, however, was his increasing conviction that his mission in life had not been fulfilled, that such things as he had been able to accomplish might even be annulled by a conservative successor. This feeling, bordering perhaps on a touch of megalomania, might have been encouraged by the tremendous acclaim that he had received from both royalty and mobs on his European visit in 1910. Furthermore, and greatly to the distress of some of his intimates, he had veered sharply to the left and was actually endorsing the highly controversial issue of Initiative, Referendum, and Recall, by which the voters of a state would be empowered to reverse judicial decisions of which they disapproved.

William Roscoe Thayer wrote an interesting account of an evening with TR and Judge Robert Grant in Boston, where the three old friends met to discuss the issue of TR's candidacy. Thayer protested that the Referendum and Recall would mean the end of representative government and its substitution by the whim of the populace of the moment. But TR retorted that we had no representative government, exclaiming: "I can name forty-six senators who secured their seats and hold them by the favor of a Wall Street magnate and his associates in all parts of the country. Do you call that popular representative government?"

Thayer and Grant were so appalled by the new radicalism of their friend that they ended by urging him not to run. But he was now ready to declare his candidacy and told them: "I wish to draw into one dominant stream all the intelligent and patriotic elements in order to prepare against the social upheaval which will otherwise overwhelm us!"

It seems to me that this marks the point where the change in TR noted by Archie Butt on the ex-president's return from his triumphant tour of Europe showed that it was not for the better but, as Butt had dared to speculate, for evil. From here on TR is inclined to reveal himself as vindictive and wholly intolerant of any opposition. One had to be either with him or a deadly foe. He had, of course, always had this tendency, but now it was less and less relieved by compassion or even by his old sense of humor.

Early in 1912 Taft at last declared open war on his predecessor by labeling as political emotionalists or neurotics all those who advocated the recall of judicial decisions, and TR responded with a cry that was original with him: "My hat is in the ring!"

Root felt as strongly as Taft about the issue of recall, which he regarded as the end of constitutional government, and he poured his heart out to Robert Bacon, Morgan partner and later secretary of state:

> Theodore has gone off on a perfectly wild program, most of which he does not really believe in, although of course at this moment he thinks he does. He has a tremendous following of Populists and Socialists in both parties and all the advantage of the dissatisfaction and dislike for the rich and successful, and he is stimulating that element with all his extraordinary skill. His course has had the

effect of throwing Taft into high relief in the public mind as the representative of conservative constitutionalism. I don't think Roosevelt will succeed in getting the nomination. He will, however, succeed in so damaging Taft that he can't be elected. If Roosevelt should be nominated he could not possibly be elected. Of course, Lodge, George Meyer, Stimson and myself, who cannot possibly go with Roosevelt in his departure, have been feeling very gloomy over the situation. . . . Altogether I shall be glad to get up to the farm at Clinton under the protection of a force of accomplished liars who will say that I am not at home. In the meantime, however, I wish to fall upon your neck and weep. I wish to walk up and down in your congenial and unrestraining presence and curse and swear and say things which I would not have repeated for the world.

But Root was not to escape to his beloved farm to avoid the painful test of the Republican convention in Chicago. He was to be its chairman.

Arguments about who cheated whom out of what in that convention continue to this day. It presents a sorry picture of democracy in action. The bickerings are endless over Root's rulings as chairman as to whether challenged delegates should be allowed to vote on issues prior to the decision as to their qualification, and whether delegates who were present but refused to vote could be represented by their alternates, but Philip Jessup, in his excellent life of Root, concludes: "Under ordinary circumstances, a mere quarrel about a parliamentary ruling would have amounted to little; in this convention, due to the personality of Roosevelt, all of these incidents were cumulative and were seized upon to sustain the charges of fraud and theft and to justify the Bull Moose bolt."

Root always maintained that he had acted scrupulously and fairly on every issue, and it can certainly be argued that TR would not have won even if granted his disputed votes, but the whole matter is so cloaked in lies and subterfuge that it is not possible to make a valid assessment. At any rate, Taft was nominated, and Roosevelt, convinced that he had been cheated out of victory, felt morally released to head a third party.

Root moaned to a friend: "I care more for one button on Theodore Roosevelt's waistcoat than for Taft's whole body."

The progressives who now abandoned the

Republican Party in Chicago formed their own independent party, to be called the Bull Moose, and promptly nominated Roosevelt who responded with his famous cry, "We stand at Armageddon and we battle for the Lord!"

Nobody had been more appalled by TR's challenge of Taft than Lodge, who had written to his old and dearest friend: "I have had my share of mishaps in politics, but I never thought that any situation could arise which could have made me as miserably unhappy as I have been during the past week." But Lodge maintained his loyalty to the party despite all, and Roosevelt, uncharacteristically, forgave him. Perhaps it was because it was the deepest friendship of Roosevelt's life, and perhaps because Lodge never said or did anything that his friend could take as personally disloyal. But with Root it was different. TR would not even speak to Root for four years, and he described him as the kind of lawyer who was paid by mighty corporations to permit them to do what the law forbids and yet avoid the penalty that might otherwise attend technical violations of the law. But, of course, Roosevelt was convinced that Root had used his chairmanship to rig a false nomination and deserved jail!

TR embarked on a vigorous campaign that was characterized by statements showing his continuing swing to the left. Antitrust suits were no longer enough; his stand was what he had said a year earlier: "The effort at prohibiting all combinations has substantially failed. The way out lies, not in attempting to prevent such combinations, but in completely controlling them in the interest of the public welfare." But an attempt on his life interrupted his western tour and sent him home to Sagamore to await the election.

A would-be assassin fired a bullet into his chest as he was approaching the podium to make a speech in Milwaukee. The missile was deflected from a fatal effect by the contents of his breast pocket. "As I did not cough blood," he explained later, "I was pretty sure the wound was not a fatal one." Continuing his progress to the platform he told his horror-stricken audience: "Friends, I shall ask you to be as quiet as possible. I don't know whether you fully understand that I have just been shot; but it takes more than that to kill a bull moose. . . . The bullet is in me now, so I cannot make a very long speech, but I will try my best." He insisted on finishing his address before the doctors rushed him to the hospital. It was the most dramatic performance of a lifetime of dramatic performances. He may even have enjoyed it.

He wanted to continue the campaign, but Edith arrived at the hospital and took him firmly home to convalesce. There was no gainsaying her when she was convinced something was necessary for his health. The aides were amused at how docilely their fiery chief took his orders from her, and the public sympathy aroused by the event was probably worth more votes than any campaign would have brought in.

Nothing, however, could save a party fatally split in two. Woodrow Wilson won with more than six million votes; Roosevelt polled four and Taft only three and a half. TR had handed the nation over to the Democrats and become the greatest mugwump in Republican history. It is interesting to note that James Bryce, the British historian who showed in his great work, *The American Commonwealth*, that he understood our political system to the core and who was a close friend of TR, said that what Roosevelt had really resented in the mugwumps who had bolted the party in 1884 was that they had impeached his own righteousness and classed him with the politicians. One wonders if he ever had doubts about the bolters of 1912. But doubting, of course, was not his habit. At least not overt doubting.

What he may have done to his party may still affect it to this day. Has the Republican Party ever really recovered the liberal wing which abandoned it to follow TR in 1912?

As Africa had provided the needed distraction for TR after leaving the White House in 1909, so did South America offer an alternative challenge after the fiasco of the Bull Moose campaign. There was a large river in Brazil, appropriately called the River Doubt, which headed north toward the equatorial rain forest and was supposed to join the Amazon in some uncharted dense jungle area. It was this that TR and his son Kermit proposed to explore in the company of some scientists on an expedition sponsored by the American Museum of Natural History and the government of Brazil.

It was by no means an easy undertaking, particularly for a man who, if only fifty-five, had a number of physical things wrong with him, including a game leg from an injury in a street crash back in 1902. The party encountered poisonous snakes, ravenous termites, carnivorous ants, bloodsucking vampire bats, and piranhas. Fortunately the latter were good to eat. Because of the rapids they often had to proceed slowly along the banks of the river, through the steaming jungle, and this of course entailed exhausting portage of canoes and supplies.

To make matters worse, the trip took much longer than planned; supplies ran short, and illness plagued the travelers. One of their bearers was drowned; another was murdered by a man who ran amok and disappeared into the jungle. TR became seriously ill when he damaged his bad leg; he lay feverishly in his dugout reciting over and over: "In Xanadu did Kubla Khan a stately pleasure dome decree." He pleaded with the others to leave him to die and save themselves as best they could, but obviously none of the party would consent to this, and ultimately they were rescued by running into a group of rubber tappers. As TR described his ordeal for the readers of *Scribner's Magazine*:

It is not ideal for a sick man to spend the hottest hours of the day stretched on the boxes in the bottom of a small open dugout, under the well nigh intolerable heat of the torrid sun of the mid-tropics, varied by blinding, drenching downpours of rain.

Shortly after his return he was faced with

the outbreak of what would become World War I. It was to provide him with the final five-year battle of his own life: his passionate opposition to everything that Woodrow Wilson did, wrote, and said, before, during, and after the direct military involvement of the United States in the conflict.

Sixteen

If the election returns of 1912 proved anything it was that the old guard still ruled the Republican Party. The progressives who had bolted to support Roosevelt faded away, and even TR, after refusing their reoffered nomination four years later, not only because they had lost their following but because he found them too wildly radical, rejoined his old party. It was once again a united conservative body, as would be affirmed by its presidents from 1921 to 1933, and it preferred to lose the election in 1912 to winning it with TR. But it was still clear that had Roosevelt won the Republican nomination in that year, he would have defeated Wilson.

What, then, were the issues between the Democrats and the Bull Moosers, between a progressive Roosevelt and a progressive Wilson? Very few. As William Allen White put it: "Between the New Nationalism and the New Freedom was that fantastic imaginary gulf that has always existed between tweedle-dum and tweedle-dee." Their very similarity may have caused their leaders to invent issues and to misrepresent each other.

There was, however, a philosophic difference between Wilson's and Roosevelt's attitudes toward the trusts, and one that may have epitomized the basic difference between the characters of the two men.

Roosevelt tended to favor the giant corporations. He admired their force and orderly organization; he saw them as essential to the growth of a great industrial nation, as vital components of the new century of material progress. And as a devoted advocate of military preparedness, he must have also foreseen them as the indispensable producers of warships and armaments. What he objected to — and objected to forcibly — was not their size but their too frequent wickedness. *That* had to be policed by a national government stronger than the corporations themselves. The prospect of the clashing conflict and the victory of the stars and stripes was agreeable to the hero of San Juan Hill.

Wilson, the reflective scholar, the former president of Princeton, saw the business picture through a different lens. To him the mammoth size of the trusts was an evil in itself, a factor that stifled competition and shut the small guy out of the market. He wanted every man, so to speak, to have his chance; he wanted to open the business arena to new enterprises that might initially lack the capital held by the established ones. If Roosevelt believed in laissez-faire, subject to government regulation of what he deemed antisocial behavior — exploitation of labor and unfair business practices — Wilson believed in protecting the individual from being shut out of business by corporate monopoly. For, unlike his predecessor in office, he insisted that size did lead to monopoly and that monopoly did stifle competition.

As John Milton Cooper Jr. saw it, Roosevelt was the warrior who believed in a strong chief of state to inspire the nation as a heroic leader, and Wilson preferred the image of the leader who listened to the people to pick up his cue. Cooper put it this way:

> Roosevelt's misfortune lay in not having a war in which he could act upon his beliefs. His worst time began later, after the outbreak of World War I, which he viewed as a perfect historical occasion for his kind of heroic leadership. He knew he required a great national crisis, like Lincoln's with the Civil War, to practice his politics to the fullest. Only in such a situation could he have succeeded in rousing people and parties to self-sacrificing service and heroic action.

Wilson moved forward in his social program in his second term, despite his very narrow victory in 1916 over Charles Evan Hughes, until, to our eyes, he seemed to be anticipating the welfare state of the 1930s. It had to be galling to TR to see his own Square Deal outdone by tariff reform, workmen's compensation for those under government contract, an eight-hour day for railway workers, exclusion of the products of child labor from interstate commerce, and a big boost in income and inheritance taxes. Indeed, it began to look as if the federal government would take a principal role in aiding the disadvantaged, with all the danger, as Roosevelt saw it, of creating a society spoiled and feminized by a kind of permanent dole.

TR took querulous objection in the 1916 campaign, when he stumped for Hughes, to Wilson's statement that "you cannot worship God on an empty stomach, and you cannot be a patriot when you are starving." It was outrageous of Wilson, he strongly affirmed, to espouse a creed that failed to engender among Americans "something at least of that nobility of soul which makes men not only serve their country when they are starving, but when death has set its doom upon their faces."

The outbreak of war in Europe in the summer of 1914 found Wilson determined to maintain neutrality. He went further than many in his definition of what a true neutrality involved. "The United States must be neutral in fact as well as in name during these days which are to try men's souls." He called upon Americans to be impartial "in thought as well as in action" in order "to do what is necessary and disinterested and truly serviceable to the peace of the world."

Wilson was far from accusing Germany of being solely responsible for the conflict, and he saw the hope of the world not in an allied victory but in a deadlock between the foes. All during the war, up to the date of America's intervention, he initiated peace offers, mostly through his unofficial ambassador, Colonel House, in the vain hope of following a cease-fire with a conference that would contain neither a gloating and punishing victor nor a crushed opponent thirsting for revenge.

Roosevelt was not at first opposed to neutrality. He was deeply shocked by Germany's brutal invasion of Belgium and he admired Britain's pluck in so promptly implementing her treaty obligations and coming to the aid of her ally. When the Kaiser sent a delegate to call upon him in

New York and to convey a cheerful and flattering greeting, TR dryly reminded his caller of the close ties he had made on his European tour with King Albert of the Kaiser's violated small neighbor. But he had always harbored a certain admiration of the militant Germans, and although he considered Britain and France as two of the principal upholders of civilization on the globe, he had his own doubts about their imperial policies. Besides, the Russian despot was on the side of the allies, and this somewhat muddied their ethical superiority.

But as he read the tear-jerking accounts of the suffering Belgians and contemplated the speed of advance of the terrifyingly organized Prussian units, he came to see Wilson's concept of neutrality as "so strict as to forbid our even whispering protest against wrongdoing, lest such whispers might cause disturbance of our ease and well-being." And he became vociferously anxious for his country to take a more heroic stand. He was soon telling friends that "Germany is absolutely wrong."

Only a few months after the start of the war in July Roosevelt was claiming that if he had been president, he would have come to the aid of Belgium. "I should have acted on the thirtieth or thirty-first of July, as head of a signatory power of the Hague treaties, calling attention to the guaranty of Belgium's neutrality and saying that I accepted the treaties as imposing a serious obligation which I expected not only the United States but all other neutral nations to join in enforcing." He added later that such action "might very possibly have resulted in putting a stop to the war or in localizing or narrowly circumscribing its area."

Of course, this was grossly untrue, for we have seen what his real attitude had been in the summer months of 1914. Had he reached the point where he could actually delude himself that he was telling the truth? One cannot but speculate that what TR really minded about Wilson was that he occupied center stage in a world drama that seemed to have been written for just such an actor as his predecessor. It was he, TR, who should have been the hero of the script now called for; it was a role for the Rough Rider, for the man who had built the great canal, who had engineered peace in the Far East, who had confronted the criminals in the streets of New York and faced the charging elephant and lion in Kenya! And what did we have instead? A dry scholar, a university don, a man who had never heard a shot fired in anger!

TR went so far as to write, in a letter to Rudyard Kipling, whose jungle tales he admired despite their anthropomorphizing of animals, a habit he much deplored, that Wilson's family had fought on neither side in the Civil War. Did he wish to cover the wartime president with the shame of his own father who had bought a substitute in the earlier conflict? Yet he went on to add: "I have explained to my four sons that, if there is a war during their lifetime, I wish them to be in a position to explain why they did go to it and not why they did not go to it."

He announced prior to the Republican convention of 1916: "It would be a mistake to nominate me unless the country has in its mood something of the heroic — unless it feels not only devotion to ideals but the purpose measurably to realize those ideals in action."

Evidently the country did not feel so inclined, for Hughes, whom TR described as "a man somewhat in the Wilson type" and a "bearded iceberg," became the candidate, running without challenging the Democratic endorsement of Wilson as the man who had kept us out of the war.

Roosevelt is said to have gone so far as to have offered Elihu Root his old job as secretary of state if he was nominated and elected, but Root declined. He hoped, apparently, for the nomination himself. "Root had a chance to be Warwick," TR sneered, "but he threw it away because he wanted to be king, which was impossible."

Roosevelt, during the campaigns and after, continued his attacks on Wilson, hitting him again and again on two points: his failure to protest and retaliate sufficiently over the German submarine attacks on neutral shipping and on Allied nonwar vessels carrying neutrals, and for inadequate military preparation. His language became increasingly intemperate. He made merciless fun of Wilson's statement that there was such a thing as being too proud to fight; he accused him, in his reprimands to Germany, of shaking "his fist and then his finger," and he sneered at his ideal of peace without victory:

> Peace without victory is the natural ideal of the man who is too proud to fight. It is spurned by all men of lofty soul, by all men fit to call themselves fellow-citizens of Washington and Lincoln or of the war-worn fighters who followed Grant and Lee.

And listen to his play on the name

"Shadow Lawn," the Frank Woolworth estate in New Jersey loaned to Wilson as a summer White House in 1916:

There should be shadows now at Shadow Lawn, the shadows of the men, women and children who have risen from the ooze of the ocean bottom and from graves in foreign lands: the shadows of the helpless whom Mr. Wilson did not dare protect lest he should have to face danger, the shadows of babies gasping pitifully as they sank under the waves, the shadows of women outraged and slain by bandits. . . .

When Germany's desperate decision to resume unrestricted submarine warfare in the hope that, even if it brought America into the war, the Allies could be knocked out before new troops could be brought across the Atlantic, and Wilson was at last compelled to ask Congress for a declaration of war, Roosevelt tried to make up to the president for some of the terrible things he had said:

Mr. President, what I have said and thought and what others have said and thought, is all dust in a windy street, if now we can make your message good. Of course, it amounts to nothing if we cannot make it good. But if we can translate it into fact, then it will rank as a great state paper, with the great state papers of Washington and Lincoln. Now all that I ask is that I be allowed to do all that is in me to help make good this speech of yours — to help get the nation to act, so as to justify and live up to the speech, and the declaration of war that followed.

TR was determined to raise a company similar to the Rough Riders in 1898 and take it to France. To accomplish this he decided to appeal to the president himself. The interview was of course granted, and TR did his best to be pleasant. Wilson was cordial enough but noncommittal. He warned Roosevelt that the days of the charge of the Light Brigade were over and that modern warfare was a highly technical and not a romantic business. TR, voicing his discouragement to Wilson's friend and adviser Colonel House afterward, said: "After all, I'm only asking to be allowed to die." House is supposed to have replied: "Oh? Did you make that quite clear to the President?"

Permission to form the regiment was, of

course, denied. The army brass hardly wished to be saddled with an independent-minded and bossy ex-president and a troop of his admiring Rough Riders in the complicated and ugly business of trench warfare. Besides, Roosevelt himself was in no shape to assume any sort of command at the front; he was half-blind, overweight, and rheumatic, and would be dead in another two years.

It remained for him to supervise the departure of all his family overseas. The four sons were more than eager to go; all were Roosevelts to the core. Kermit was afraid the American armed forces would not get him into combat fast enough; he enlisted in the English army and was later given the British War Cross for gallantry in action as commander of a light-armored motor battery in the offensive against the Turks in Iraq.

Archibald ("Archie") and Theodore Jr. ("Ted") fought more conventionally as American officers in the trenches during the whole of the American involvement there. Archie was severely wounded thrice, and Ted was gassed. Both survived, however, to fight in World War II, and Archie received the Croix de Guerre. Quentin joined the army air force and was shot down behind enemy lines, the sole casualty of the family. Ethel became a nurse in France.

But TR's determination that all Roosevelts must serve in combat was not confined to his immediate family. On a visit to Washington he stayed at the house of his distant cousin and nephew-in-law, Franklin, who occupied, as assistant secretary of the navy, the same position that TR had at the outbreak of the Spanish-American War and also had a large family. TR greatly irritated his niece Eleanor by urging Franklin to follow in his footsteps, resign his office, and go to war, which Franklin, in his important military position, was certainly under no moral compulsion to do, though he had, according to Eleanor, already offered his resignation to the president and been refused. Did TR feel that his father's failure to serve in the army in the Civil War had placed every Roosevelt under a special duty to fight?

If that were so, the duty was again fulfilled by his three surviving sons twenty-three years later in World War II. Archie, as a lieutenant colonel in charge of a battalion in New Guinea, had been asked to pinpoint Japanese placements. He took a boat into the open water in full view of enemy gunners, and here is how Edward J. Renehan Jr.

describes what happened:

As the cannon boomed away at him,
Archie stood calmly on the deck of his
little craft with binoculars and a map,
marking down the flash points as they revealed themselves. On one of these excursions Archie noticed a frightened
enlisted man hunkered down in the
bottom of the boat saying a prayer.
"Don't worry," he told the boy, "you're
safe with me. I was wounded three times
in the last war, and that's a lucky charm."

Ted, a brigadier general, participated in
the invasion of Normandy with his son, another Quentin, and died a few weeks later of
a heart attack at the front. Kermit, suffering
from depression and alcoholism, died by his
own hand in Alaska, but in uniform.

As the First World War dragged on and
the carnage seemed never to end, TR began
grimly to envisage the possibility that he
might lose all his sons in it. At last he
showed a softening in his requirement that
everyone should remain permanently in
battle stations, as exemplified in this appeal
to Archie:

Of course, we wish you to get into the

fighting in the line. That is the first thing to be done; you would never be happy if you hadn't done it, and neither would I in your place. If *after* you have been in the fighting line — whether for a short or long term matters not — you are offered a staff job *in which you can be more useful,* it would then be foolish to refuse it merely because it was less dangerous.

Archie must have sensed that this was a weak moment of his father's, for he never acted on it.

The death of Quentin, shortly before the end of the war, was a devastating blow to the Roosevelts. TR has been described as sitting desolate on the porch at Sagamore, murmuring over and over, "Poor Quinikins! Poor Quinikins!" But he could still write proudly to an old Rough Rider friend, Robert Ferguson:

It is bitter that the young should die, but there are things worse than death; for nothing under heaven would I have had my sons act otherwise than as they acted. They have done pretty well, haven't they? Quentin killed, dying as a war hawk should . . . over the enemy's lines. Archie crippled, and given the French war cross for gallantry. Ted gassed once . . . and cited for conspicuous gallantry. Kermit with the British military cross, and now under Pershing.

His own end was near, though he did not suspect it. Mrs. Winthrop Chanler, an old friend, visited him in the hospital. She wrote of his last days having been darkened by political defeat, embittered by inaction and hatred of Wilson. And then:

I saw him in the hospital shortly before the end came; he did not think it was near. As I was about to say good-bye he held my hand and said, very seriously, but with none of his old gay fire, "I seem pretty low now, but I shall get better. I cannot go without having done something to that old gray skunk in the White House."

She wondered what would be his ultimate reputation in history. "Clio is biting her pencil while she looks for the final word."

He did get out of the hospital but only to die in Sagamore in his sleep a few days later, just after the New Year of 1919, at the age of sixty. Archie cabled his brothers: "The old lion is dead."

Did he believe in another life? We only know that he once wrote Holmes that we cannot tell what happens afterward: "I have no desire before my time has come to go out into the everlasting darkness." It only mattered that there should be survivors "to whom it will be a pleasure to think well of us when we are gone."

Milestones

1858 Born in New York City, son of Theodore Roosevelt and Martha Bulloch Roosevelt.

1858 In United States, John Brown raids Harpers Ferry; is captured and hanged.

1861 U.S. Civil War begun when Confederates fire on Fort Sumter.

1863 French conquer Mexico City; Archduke Maximilian emperor.

1865 Lee's surrender at Appomattox ends U.S. Civil War. Lincoln assassinated.

1866 Austro-Prussian War.

1867 Karl Marx writes *Das Kapital*. French leave Mexico. United States buys Alaska.

1869 Suez Canal opens.

1871 Franco-Prussian War ends with French surrender. German empire established. Italy united with Rome as capital.

1876 In United States, Custer's Last Stand occurs at Little Bighorn.

1878 In United States, Knights of Labor

establish first successful national union.

1880 Graduated Harvard College. Married Alice Lee.

1881 Assassinations of Garfield and Czar Alexander II of Russia.

1881–82 Attended Columbia Law School.

1882–84 Served three terms as New York State assemblyman.

1884 Death of Alice Lee Roosevelt.

1884 Invested in cattle ranch in Badlands, Dakota Territory.

1884 Delegate to Republican presidential convention in Chicago. Supported James G. Blaine when Blaine received the nomination despite Roosevelt's opposition.

1886 Defeated as a candidate for mayoralty of New York City. Married Edith Carow.

1888 Wilhelm II emperor of Germany.

1889–95 Member of Civil Service Commission.

1893 Labour Party established in England.

1894 Pullman strike in Chicago led by Eugene V. Debs.

1895–96 President of New York City's Police Commission.

1897–98 Assistant secretary of the navy.

1898 In Cuba as colonel of the "Rough Riders."

1898 United States annexes Hawaii.

1898–99 Spanish-American War. United States acquires Puerto Rico, Guam and the Philippines as colonies.

1899–1900 Governor of New York.

1899–1902 Boer War in South Africa.

1900 Boxer Rebellion in China.

1901 Vice president of the United States.

1901–9 President of the United States.

1902 United States acquires control of the Panama Canal Zone.

1904–5 Russo-Japanese War.

1907 J. P. Morgan averts run on American banks.

1910 African safari.

1912 Unsuccessful campaign for presidency as nominee of the Bull Moose Party.

1914–18 World War I.

1919 Treaty of Versailles.

1919 Death of Theodore Roosevelt.

Selected Bibliography

I have listed only the works of particular value to this study.

Adams, James Truslow. *The Epic of America*. Boston: Little, Brown, 1931.

Beale, Howard K. *Theodore Roosevelt and His Rise to World Power*. Baltimore: Johns Hopkins Press, 1956.

Blum, John Morton. *The Republican Roosevelt*. Cambridge: Harvard University Press, 1977.

Brands, H. W. *TR, The Last Romantic*. New York: Basic Books, 1997.

Busch, Noel F. *The Story of Theodore Roosevelt and His Influence on Our Times*. New York: Reynal & Co., 1963.

Cooper, John Milton Jr. *The Warrior and the Priest*. Cambridge: Belknap Press/Harvard University, 1983.

Einstein, Lewis. *Roosevelt, His Mind in Action*. Boston: Houghton Mifflin, 1930.

Graham, Frank Jr. *Man's Dominion: The Story of Conservation in America*. New York: M. Evans & Co., 1972.

Harbaugh, William Henry. *Power and Re-*

sponsibility: The Life and Times of Theodore Roosevelt. New York: Farrar, Straus & Cudahy, 1961.

Jessup, Philip. *Elihu Root.* New York: Dodd Mead & Co., 1938.

McCullough, David. *Mornings on Horseback.* New York: Simon & Schuster, 1982.

Miller, Nathan. *Theodore Roosevelt.* New York: William Morrow, 1992.

Morris, Edmund. *The Rise of Theodore Roosevelt.* New York: Coward, McCann & Geoghegan, 1979.

Pearson, Edmund Lester. *Theodore Roosevelt.* New York: Macmillan, 1920.

Pinchot, Gifford. *Breaking New Ground.* New York: Harcourt, Brace & World, 1947.

Pringle, Henry F. *The Life and Times of William Howard Taft.* New York: Farrar & Rinehart, 1939.

————. *Theodore Roosevelt.* New York: Blue Ribbon Books, 1931.

Renehan, Edward J. Jr. *The Lion's Pride.* New York: Oxford University Press, 1998.

Roosevelt, Theodore. *An Autobiography.* New York: Charles Scribner's Sons, 1920.

————. *The Letters of Theodore Roosevelt.*

Edited by Elting Morison. Vols. 1–6.
Cambridge: Harvard University Press,
1951.

———. *The Winning of the West*. New York:
Current Literature Publishing Co.,
1906.

Roosevelt, Theodore, and Henry Cabot
Lodge. *Selections from the Correspon-
dence*. New York: Charles Scribner's
Sons, 1925.

Thayer, William Roscoe. *Theodore Roosevelt:
An Intimate Biography*. Boston:
Houghton Mifflin, 1919.

Wagenknecht, Edward. *The Seven Worlds of
Theodore Roosevelt*. New York:
Longmans Green, 1958.

About the Author

Louis Auchincloss is a highly renowned novelist, literary critic, and historian. The author of more than fifty books, including *The Rector of Justin*, *The House of Five Talents*, and *The Atonement*, he is the former president of the American Academy of Arts and Letters. He lives in New York City.

The employees of Thorndike Press hope you have enjoyed this Large Print book. All our Large Print titles are designed for easy reading, and all our books are made to last. Other Thorndike Press Large Print books are available at your library, through selected bookstores, or directly from us.

For information about titles, please call:

(800) 223-1244
(800) 223-6121

To share your comments, please write:

Publisher
Thorndike Press
295 Kennedy Memorial Drive
Waterville, ME 04901